D0773425

BEING
TRANSFORMED:
AN INNER WAY
OF SPIRITUAL GROWTH

POTENTIALS
GUIDES FOR PRODUCTIVE LIVING

Wayne E. Oates, General Editor

BEING TRANSFORMED: AN INNER WAY OF SPIRITUAL GROWTH

by

EDWARD E. THORNTON

THE WESTMINSTER PRESS
Philadelphia

Book Design by Alice Derr

First edition

Published by The Westminster Press ®
Philadelphia, Pennsylvania

PRINTED IN THE UNITED STATES OF AMERICA
9 8 7 6 5 4 3 2 1

Library of Congress Cataloging in Publication Data

Thornton, Edward E.
    Being transformed, an inner way of spiritual growth.

    (Potentials)
    1. Spiritual life—Baptist authors. 2. Thornton,
Edward E. I. Title. II. Series.
BV4501.2.T5147 1984   248.4'861   83-27331
ISBN 0-664-24523-4 (pbk.)

To
Betty

Contents

Foreword

The eleven books in this series, Potentials: Guides for Productive Living, speak to your condition and mine in the life we have to live today. The books are designed to ferret out the potentials you have with which to rise above rampant social and psychological problems faced by large numbers of individuals and groups. The purpose of rising above the problems is portrayed as far more than merely your own survival, merely coping, and merely "succeeding" while others fail. These books with one voice encourage you to save your own life by living with commitment to Jesus Christ, and to be a creative servant of the common good as well as your own good.

In this sense, the books are handbooks of ministry with a new emphasis: coupling your own well-being with the well-being of your neighbor. You use the tools of comfort wherewith God comforts you to be a source of strength to those around you. A conscious effort has been made by each author to keep these two dimensions of the second great commandment of our Lord Jesus Christ in harmony with each other.

The two great commandments are summarized in Luke 10:25–28: "And behold, a lawyer stood up to put him to the test, saying, 'Teacher, what shall I do to inherit eternal life?' He said to him, 'What is written in the law? How do you read?' And he answered, 'You shall love the Lord your God with all your heart, and with all your soul, and with all your strength, and with all your mind; and your neighbor as yourself.' And he said to him, 'You have answered right; do this, and you will live.' "

Underneath the two dimensions of neighbor and self there is also a persistent theme: The only way you can receive such harmony of thought and action is by the intentional re-centering of your life on the sovereignty of God and the rapid rejection of all idols that would enslave you. The theme, then, of this series of books is that these words of Jesus are the master guides both to the realization of your own potentials and to productive living in the nitty-gritty of your day's work.

The books in this series are unique, and each claims your attention separately in several ways.

First, these books address great social issues of our day, but they do so in terms of your own personal involvement in and responses to the problems. For example, the general problem of the public school system, the waste in American consumerism, the health hazards in a lack of rest and vocational burnout, the crippling effects of a defective mental outlook, and the incursion of Eastern mystical traditions into Western Christian activism are all larger-than-life issues. Yet each author translates the problem into the terms of day-to-day living and gives concrete guidelines as to what you can do about the problem.

Second, these books address the undercurrent of helplessness that overwhelming epidemic problems produce in you. The authors visualize you throwing up your hands and saying: "There is nothing *anyone* can do about it." Then they show you that this is not so, and that there are things *you* can do about it.

Third, the authors have all disciplined themselves to stay off their own soapboxes and to limit oratory about how awful the world is. They refuse to stop at gloomy diagnoses of incurable conditions. They go on to deal with your potentials for changing yourself and your world in very specific ways. They do not let you, the reader, off the hook with vague, global utterances and generalized sermons. They energize you with a sense of hope that is generated by basic information, clear decision-making, and new directions taken by you yourself.

Fourth, these books get their basic interpretations and recommendations from a careful plumbing of the depths of the power of faith in God through Jesus Christ. They are not books that leave you with the illusion that you can lift yourself and your world by pulling hard at your own bootstraps. They energize and inspire you through the hope and strength that God in Christ is making available to you through the wisdom of the Bible and the presence of the living Christ in your life. Not even this, though, is presented in a namby-pamby or trite way. You will be surprised with joy at the freshness of the applications of biblical truths which you have looked at so often that you no longer notice their meaning. You will do many "double takes" with reference to your Bible as you read these books. You will find that the Bread of Life is not too holy or too good for human nature's daily food.

For a long time I have sought for a book that makes spiritual contemplation in the inner being something that is a part of every person's hectic existence, an inner way of becoming more than the pious platitudes of mass-produced religiosity. Edward Thornton frankly lays out his own disenchantment with the rote quality of his earlier Christian experience and how he had the nerve and honesty to chuck the whole thing. Yet he did not stop there. He started rebuilding an inner life of contemplation over a period of many years. This book is a vital documentary of his pilgrimage from conformity as a way of religious life to transformation of his life through the cultivation of the Presence of God.

I cannot and would not dare try to capture in a few lines on this page the intensity and clarity of Edward Thornton's treatment of the practice of meditation in the service of loving God with your whole heart and your neighbor as yourself. He speaks of it as a way of praying with the mind in the heart and calls it the "prayer-of-the-heart." He goes far beyond the naive emotionalism of much devotional literature. He seeks not to bypass the intelligence of a person but to go on to the transformation of the mind by the wisdom of the heart in communion with God. Of all the many books I have read on meditation, this one centers down upon the very essence of the purity of heart in the adoration of God after the way of the heart of Jesus Christ.

WAYNE E. OATES

Louisville, Kentucky

Chapter 1

There Is
More Light Here

The title of this book, "Being Transformed: An Inner Way of Spiritual Growth," has already done its winnowing work. Many people, without ever handling the book or reading this opening paragraph, have decided it is not for them. You, however, are different. Something has made you take a look. I wonder what makes the difference? I suspect that somewhere in the mix of your motives is a desire for progress in your own spiritual life. Perhaps, too, you hope to benefit from traveling along for a while with someone else on that person's inner journey of spiritual growth.

Beyond hopes such as these, you are probably a practical person who wants nothing to do with fads in your religious life. A practical person wants specific solutions to problems in everyday living. I imagine that you have had a few "peak" experiences at some time in your life. By "peak" experience I mean a sense of a higher power beyond yourself, a more than normal sense of love, joy, peace, and well-being. Such a moment usually deepens religious values and whets your appetite for religious experience.

I see you also as a person who is honest with yourself—not indulging in wishful thinking or pious platitudes. In my mind's eye I see you facing up to the earthy aspects of life—its ugliness, cruelty, pain, and loss. You want wisdom and you want to care for others as well as yourself. Most likely you have had several transformations already on your life journey. You are willing, therefore, to consider the transformations that remain—particularly those which come from shifting your energies from outer to inner ways of growth.

Not Just Change, but Transformation

Change is not the same as transformation. You struggle to change yourself in so many ways, with nothing to show for it. You take two steps forward and slide three steps back. Then a transformation happens. Everything seems to change. Nothing is just as it was. Old habits that you tried to change without success just fall away. Fixed ideas that drove you without mercy evaporate. New ideas and behaviors take over—exciting, energizing, empowering. In time, however, what once was fresh becomes stale, and again you need a transformation. In the rhythms of growth you discover that mere change is not enough. From time to time you need to be transformed.

Transformation is not minor change, it is major change. It is change in condition and character: from a forgotten Cinderella to a beloved princess; from Peter denying the Christ to Peter defying the Sanhedrin. To be transformed is to be changed in form and appearance: from an ugly duckling to a lovely swan; from brokenhearted to embraced in love; from coldhearted to aflame with compassion; from alone, abandoned, to befriended by a soul mate of your own.

To be transformed is to undergo a metamorphosis. The apostle Paul appeals to us in Rom. 12:2 not to be conformed to this world but to be *metamorphized,* that is, "transformed," by the remodeling of our minds. The image in *metamorphized* is the change from caterpillar to butterfly—from ugly to beautiful, from crawling to flying, from the safety of a cocoon to the freedom of the sky, from sleeping to waking.

That God intends your transformation in form and character is clear to see. You are transformed at birth—from fetus to infant; in adolescence—from child to adult; in parenthood—from self-centered to self-giving. Yet you may be asleep to God's call to an inner transformation as well.

Inner transformation means not conforming to the ways of the present age, but (to paraphrase Rom. 12:2) being transformed by the remodeling of your mind to see clearly the will of God—what are the best, the most pleasing to God, and the most mature choices possible. Inner transformation is like waking from sleep. It is coming out of a fogbank of spiritual drowsiness into the bright sky of a Canadian high. It is remembering that you are a son or a daughter of God; that you can now see his Presence in everything. You can see yourself as you really are—made in the image of God. You can see yourself as you may become—"changed into his likeness" (II Cor. 3:18). You can enjoy the intimacy of calling God "abba." ("Abba" in the Hebrew tongue is the first name that an infant uses for the male parent. Translating this into English, you may call God "daddy.")

Searching for the Key

The verb "to transform," when applied to religious experience, almost always appears in its passive form, "to be transformed." As you awaken to the need for major change, you typically grope around, as if you were blind, in search of the key that will unlock and open you to the process of transformation.

I am reminded of the man who was searching for something

on the ground under a streetlight near his home. A friend came along and asked, "What have you lost?"

"The key to my box of treasures," said the man.

So the friend went down on his knees too, and they both looked for it.

After a time, the friend asked, "Where exactly did you drop your key?"

"In my house," was the reply.

"Then why are you looking here?" exploded the friend.

"Because," said the man, "there is more light here. It is dark inside my house."

What can we say about the man who lost the key to his treasure? Clearly he is stupid, stupid, stupid!

Yet I must come to his defense, for his case is mine as well. You see, I spent five years in my early adulthood looking for the key that would unlock me as a person under the light of the biblical languages—Hebrew and Greek.

I was certain that if I could discover the original text of the Scriptures I would find final answers to all my questions about life. After two years of Hebrew and four years of Greek I gave up the search for absolute answers. I found that the translation of nearly every passage of Scripture requires translators—human beings like me—to compare scores of ancient manuscripts, to make judgments as to the age, reliability, and fitness of variant texts, and in that way to shape the Greek or Hebrew text from which other translators make judgments about the words and idioms to use in English versions.

Two options remained: to reject biblical authority, or to trust the Holy Spirit to have guided hundreds of scribes and translators through the centuries and, in particular, to have guided the textual experts who put together the Hebrew or

Greek texts. Then I needed to trust the same Spirit to guide me in understanding and living the truth myself.

Well, there was the rub. The Holy Spirit had never been easy for me to conjure up. And when I experienced the Spirit—as I did a few times in growing up—the message seldom included Scriptures in any direct way. The Spirit mostly gave joy in being alive, and courage to live by faith—doing without absolute answers. So, what do you do? I could not reject biblical authority and I could not really get the answers I wanted from prayer and waiting on the Spirit. After a while, therefore, I just wandered away from the puzzle and stopped paying much attention to it at all.

Before long, I found another streetlight. This time it was the behavioral sciences. Here at last was light that was really light! These authorities were scientists. They had spent lifetimes exploring the dark depths of unconscious mental processes. At last I was on a path that would lead me to the answers to my personal questions. Given time and enough research, we would understand the mysteries of the human psyche. We would be able to harmonize ancient wisdom and modern scientific truth about people and about life. We would have a unified theory of how people are put together, what makes us behave as we do, how to motivate loving behavior, and how, at last, to bring in the kingdom of God!

You must give me credit for sticking power. I stayed on my hands and knees under the streetlight of the behavioral sciences for twenty-two years. I was not praying on my hands and knees, but I was searching. How I was searching! I was in a wilderness—both wandering and learning. And, I was changing. I was getting comfortable with myself—shadows and all. I was learning to be emotionally honest. In time I discovered that I could be of real help to other people who were struggling to survive in the wilderness too. Moreover, I was loyal to my early vision: the twin lights of biblical revelation and behavioral science would lead in time to the kingdom of God—"on earth as it is in heaven."

This is my hands-and-knees era. It filled nearly a half century, for it came to an end when I was forty-seven years of age. Suppose you were to fill in the blanks for your story. What would you say? Perhaps that you hunted under the streetlight of traditional religious beliefs and practices? Perhaps under the light of conversion experiences—a whole series of them, like consciousness-expanding drugs, human rights crusades, and Oriental mysticism? Maybe your light has been a down-to-earth, practical realism—keeping clear of cults and fads. There are so many ways, so many streetlights, but all of them have one thing in common. They save us from the fear of going inside our own house.

Understandable though it is that you look under a streetlight for a key that you lost in your own house, the fact remains that you will never find the key outdoors—no matter how bright the light may be. Eventually you must go inside— into the dark.

You may find a friend who will go in with you, a friend who, it is hoped, has explored some dark houses before. Without such a friend, you must go alone, groping and stumbling, but learning slowly to feel your way around until the key is found.

I would like to be one such friend for you. I am writing this book as a guide for exploring the dark inside where you are most likely to find the key to your greatest treasures. The key is not in this book. It is not in me. The key is in you, for *the key is your own true self.*

No two keys are the same. My key will not open your treasures. You must find your own key. The most I or anyone else can do for you is to calm some of your fears about going in after it. Perhaps, also, I can awaken your desire to be fully alive to your true self, to overcome lack of interest in looking for the key to your inner riches and to face the dangers together. So let us consider first *lack of interest* in the search and secondly *dangers* along the way.

Lack of Interest in the Search

Being True to Yourself

I want to be clear that I am not now dividing the sheep and the goats. Seekers on the inner way are not the sheep, with uninterested ones the goats. Lack of interest in inner ways of seeking may be for you a necessary step on the way to finding your true self. You may find the key to your treasure in intellectual work, in the service of others, or in the strenuous inner work of contemplation. Strange as it may seem, the key for you may be in loyalty to yourself as a pilgrim of the outer way rather than of the inner way. The dark place for you may be staying outside the spiritually "in" ways of seeking.

What I am saying here may have to do with personality types. At this point we do not know enough to prescribe specific methods of spiritual growth for particular types of persons. Given the darkness that surrounds the topic, I encourage you to be true to yourself, trusting also the discovery of Jeremiah:

> You will seek me and find me;
> when you seek me with all your heart.
> (Jer. 29:13)

Developmental Factors

Lack of interest in new ways of spiritual growth may be due to the success of old ways already well set. During the years I was investing in psychotherapy as a way of finding myself I had no interest in traditional ways of Christian spirituality. In fact, I was hard against them. I remember well meeting Dr. Harmon Bro, a noted psychotherapist and Christian mystic. I greeted him with the question: "What is a good therapist like you doing messing around with mysticism?" He got even some years later when I called to ask him to write an article on Christian mysticism for a journal I was editing. There was a long pause over the phone after I said what I wanted of him, after which he asked: "What's a good therapist like you doing messing around with mysticism?" During the years that had passed, summer had given way to fall in the seasons of my life. The way that was right for me in the summer of my life was wrong for the fall. And so it may be for you. Developmental factors, the stage of your life journey, may require you to be uninterested in the inner way today while ready tomorrow.

Loyalty to Models and Mentors

Another factor in lack of interest may be loyalty to the models and mentors of your youth. When I was a teenager the writings of Glenn Clark started me on the inner way of spirituality. Unfortunately, I used the piety I learned then to hide a weak sense of myself. By the time I entered a theological seminary, I was using prayer and devotional reading to avoid facing my sexual needs, my angers, and my selfishness.

In the seminary I found new models and a special mentor. In them I saw new psychological disciplines for inner growth and I began to see the weakness in the old pietistic model. I remember well exactly where I was sitting in the seminary chapel on a fateful day. It was the day I made the most important decision about my spiritual life during my seminary years. I decided to stop doing personal prayer and devotional reading altogether! I felt I had to stop in order to become honest with God. I was certain that being honest with myself and learning psychological ways of loving my neighbor was the only way—in my condition at that time—the only way I could love God with a whole heart. I could not then have been more uninterested in the inner way of Christian spirituality.

Discouragement from Past Failures

Discouragement may breed lack of interest. You may try Christian spirituality with a strong sense of readiness. You may seek to find your true self, to gain a sense of inner peace, to get free to be open to others, compassionate and spontaneously joyful. You find a guide, follow instruction faithfully, but nothing really changes—except for the worse. You become more upset because the new way is not working. You are less at peace than ever, more moody and miserable. The outcome is predictable: you give up on the spiritual way. You are fortunate if you do not carry away a heavy sense of failure and a fear of risking the journey another time. In the meantime your lack of interest may be a needed protection against being hurt.

Avoiding Growing Pains

The discouragement syndrome sets in near the end of every stage of normal growth. You give up the innocence of childhood for the freedoms of adolescence only to find in time that freedom from commitments is a new bondage. The growing pains of young adults struggling to choose values, mates, and vocations are intense. The lust for shortcuts is powerful. The inner way of spiritual growth may fascinate you until you see that spiritual growth is slow and painful—just like growing up from child to youth, from youth to adult.

Dangers on the Journey

Once the teachable time has come and readiness for the inner way of spiritual growth is ripe, new obstacles appear. These are the fears of danger along the way, and to these we turn next.

Magical Thinking

Magical thinking is the only kind of thinking you can do as a child. You make sense out of the world by seeing everything as if you were yourself the center of the universe. When your best friend moves to another city, you feel as if God ordered this event to punish you. Let your parents be unaware of your need for attention and you feel that they have read your angry mind and are getting even by ignoring you.

Slowly and painfully you face up to the many forces in your chum's world beyond God's need to punish you and the many problems your parents have besides a bothersome kid. Then you grow up and consider turning to prayer again. You have long since stopped thinking magically about most things, but suddenly you feel as if you are on center stage in a cosmic drama once again. You know better, but moving back toward an intimate relationship with God triggers childish desires to be God's favorite, to be immune to troubles, and to be able to get God to do what you want by using just the right formula in prayer.

As a young person, I used prayer as a kind of Aladdin's lamp. Unfortunately for me, when I rubbed the Aladdin's lamp of prayer, many of my requests seemed to be granted. So I kept up the magic ritual until that fateful day in a seminary chapel when I decided not to pray privately at all.

One time when I was about twelve years of age, for example, a car full of us boys was leaving a Y-league basketball tournament, having a good time and telling dirty stories. My conscience bothered me about it, so I rubbed the Aladdin's lamp in prayer. The genie came and I asked what I should do about dirty stories. And the genie said, "Get out of the basketball league." So, of course, I did. Unwittingly, I also dropped out of chumship, rationalized a loner life-style and a self-righteous attitude, got stuck in immaturity and conventional morality, and thereby threw up quite a roadblock in my spiritual progress.

I could not have known until many years later that my genie was not the Holy Spirit but was instead my own tyrannical conscience formed in a Victorian, pietistic clan and church. Little wonder that the awakening of an appetite for prayer in mid-life threatened to awaken also the sleeping dogs of tyrannical conscience, conventional morality, emotional immaturity, and magical thinking.

Today I see that the greater danger is not sliding back into the magical thinking of childhood innocence, but failing, as an adult, to move forward into a second childhood, a second naiveté. Magical thinking and the experience of mystery are totally different. They must not be confused with each other in adult experience. Magical thinking is a way of trying to get control over the world. Awareness of mystery inspires awe and wonder, humility before the universe, and a willingness to flow with the tides of life rather than to try to dam them up with beach sand.

The real danger, then, may be a refusal to risk the inner way of spiritual growth when the time has come to do so. Not to open yourself to becoming "as a child" may block your growth as an adult rather than, as you may fear, putting you on a greased slide back into childishness. Could this be part of what Jesus had in mind when he said, "Whoever does not receive the kingdom of God like a child shall not enter it" (Luke 18:17)?

Spiritual Snobbery

Spiritual snobbery raises its proud head wherever people travel the inner way of spiritual growth. A tragic split happened in the early church. Theologians divided the guidelines for spiritual growth into commands and counsels and in so doing they split Christians into first- and second-class citizens in one blow. Commandments were for the laity, but the "counsels of perfection" were for the clergy, for monks and religious. By following the "way of perfection" men and women in Holy Orders believed they could progress step by step on an endless ascent toward purity, wisdom, and a final union with God. Post-Vatican II Roman Catholicism is changing all of this, however, but many Catholics (and Protestants) are deeply infected with the disease of spiritual snobbery.

Protestants were not immune. Trying to account for the mystery of the difference between those who awoke with desire for God and those who remained spiritually asleep throughout life, their theologians came up with a doctrine of election. Divine choice, not human choice, determined the spiritual fate of everyone. Theoretically no basis remains for spiritual pride because the elect are awake to God not by their own virtue or choice but by God's action alone. Unhappily, the disease of spiritual snobbery was contagious and reappeared in Protestantism as pietistic perfectionism. As you consider the inner way of spiritual growth, remember that a strong skepticism of spiritual pride will inoculate you against the snobbery disease.

Going off the Deep End

Closely related to spiritual snobbery is the danger of going off the deep end. If you go off the deep end, you become impractical and unrealistic about the problems of everyday living. One man left a prayer retreat excited by the discovery that in a deeply relaxed state one's hands emit vibrations that relieve joint pains when the hands surround an affected joint. A few days later his six-year-old son hurt his foot. Holding the boy on his lap, the father closed his eyes, began a relaxation exercise, and cupped the lad's foot with his hands. After watching his father's blank face and strange gestures, the boy looked up at him and whispered, "Dad, this is ridiculous!" You need only one solid confrontation like this remark of the six-year-old to come back to earth and make the practical judgments needed to set proper limits around the times, places, and uses of any newly discovered spiritual "tricks."

The heart of the danger of going off the deep end is just this, that you become fascinated by the "tricks" and forget that the inner way of spiritual growth is *a way of life* and not a bag of tricks. Every teacher of the inner way warns against being turned on by the psychic fireworks that explode from time to time. They excite you as they happen, but when they are past, only a puff of smoke remains. Once you decide to stay in the middle of the road of common sense, you find that meditation, for example, solves everyday problems such as headaches and sleeplessness. It improves concentration in reading, sewing, carpentering, or fixing broken toasters. Over a period of time it relieves much of your impatience, indecision, and worrying.

Deciding to open yourself to the Spirit, to risk receiving guidance from beyond, arouses anxiety that is not altogether allayed by talking about practical realism. For several years I opened myself to direct guidance from the Spirit only in a guarded way. Somewhere in the dim recesses of memory were stories of the Oxford movement, where educated persons trained themselves to act on impulse whenever they received an impression from the Spirit. I could see myself getting up from prayer to make a fool of myself in one way or another day after day. The chance of being laughed at was less of a problem to me than the loss of control over my own behavior. Then one day a bit of simple common sense dawned on me: if the Spirit wants me to do something foolish, *the Spirit will not mind repeating the instructions.* I do not need to act impulsively. I only need to act obediently—once the guidance has been repeated so that it is clear, and once I have had time to check it out in the community of faith.

Checking out impressions about divine guidance in your community of faith enables you to spot temptations other than impulsivity, such as overdramatization and self-display, inviting psychological martyrdom, and hurting others by embarrassing them.

Going Public Too Soon

Perhaps the wisest safeguard for you as a new traveler on the inner way of spiritual growth is to decide to remain private about your spiritual journey for several years. I took this advice in 1973, choosing to follow the model of the apostle Paul, who left the Damascus road experience and "went away into Arabia" (Gal. 1:17) for several years before going public with his conversion story, his mission work, or his writings about the life of faith. I led my first retreat on Christian Meditation and the Prayer-of-the-Heart exactly six years after a transforming moment in March of 1973. I would like to share my story now because it is a story of fighting fears on a spiritual journey as well as a story of being given a treasure I did not ask for, seek, or even—at first—want.

Going In (Even Though It's Dark Inside)

The transforming moment to which I refer came in a time of personal crisis—in the dead of night. *I experienced the Presence.* God came uninvited, unexpected, and unwelcomed. The Presence was totally absorbing. A focal problem was illuminated, and in that instant my ambition was transformed from career goals to a desire to be at one with God. For a moment I, as a branch, was one with the vine, as a lover was one in the divine heart, as an appetite was one with the feast. And the appetite continued—insatiable. The more I fed it, the stronger it grew: a longing, a hungering, a thirsting; a driving, delicious desire—a longing love for God.

The excitement of this new experience was frightening. What was this? Was it a psychic fever? A symptom of a disease of the soul? Nothing in the personality theory I knew and taught prepared me for such a change in my conscious-ness. Although I am a physician of souls, I could not heal myself. I saw no alternative but to go back into analytic psychotherapy to try to figure out what kind of disease this was. That it was a psychic disease seemed likely. At times it felt like the old days of teenage religious experience or worse, like sliding into childishness. So, before long I took my own medicine and went back into psychotherapy. And I chose a Freudian analyst who would know the pathology of the Holy Spirit when he saw it!

In due time I had my answer: I was not suffering a breakdown of mental health but was being transformed into a life-style that goes beyond mental health. What was happen-ing was not destroying my values, my relationships, or my work. Instead, it was enlarging my values, enriching my relationships, refocusing and energizing my work.

Along with psychotherapy, I was doing some work in Hatha Yoga. Yoga seemed a sensible way for a middle-aged person to exercise, so I had left a health spa, and with it the American way of abusing my body in the name of fitness. Then, in a relaxation exercise I experienced something that I came to know as a state of meditation. The meditative experience had a strong likeness to the religious experience of the Presence. I had to explore it further. To my surprise and delight, relaxation exercise and meditation prepared the way again and again for the unitive experience with God. For a while I wondered if I would have to choose between this Eastern way in which God was known and loved in immediacy—a real Presence readily renewed—and the old ways of my religious upbringing in which God was at best silent and at worst either confused with my tyrannical conscience or coldly absent.

A happy discovery solved the problem. I discovered that the most ancient form of prayer known to the Christian world is in essence *the practice of meditation in the service of loving God with a whole heart and one's neighbor as one's self.* It is a way of praying "with the mind in the heart," and so it is called *the prayer-of-the-heart.*

In the years since I made this discovery I have found that praying with the mind in the heart fuels the process of transformation. It is a way of being with your true self, with others, and with God. It fits the Pauline appeal to "be transformed by the renewal of your mind" (Rom. 12:2). Furthermore, I have found in numerous retreats and conferences and in one-to-one consultations that prayer-of-the-heart may be taught and learned. In learning and using it, people awaken to a quality of experience we may call "being transformed."

Purposes and Outcomes

This book, then, is about this inner way of spiritual growth. It comes out of my journey, informed along the way by a decade of both fighting against and flowing with the Spirit of God. It is informed also by happy discoveries of fellow pilgrims, both ancient and contemporary adventurers on the frontiers of the Spirit.

My purposes in writing are to awaken your desire for your own true self; to stir up interest in the disciplines of relaxation, centering, and contemplation; to encourage you to pay attention to the presence of the living God in the everyday business of survival; and finally to risk obedience to the Spirit as your daily bread. The point of it all is that you may actively develop yourself mentally and spiritually—growing in wisdom, compassion, and in a deep sense of well-being—of being at home in your body, mind, and spirit, and, most of all, of being at home in the One in whom "we live and move and have our being" (Acts 17:28).

If you stay with me to the end of the book, you may expect several outcomes for yourself:

1. To find that you are understood and affirmed in any skepticism you may have about the inner way of spiritual growth.

2. To experience me, as author, sharing the findings from my journey honestly, but not presuming to impose them on you or putting down the way you are choosing to travel your spiritual journey.

Indeed, I trust that these two "outcomes" have already begun to happen.

3. To become more invested in the care of your body as a part of your spirituality—perhaps giving a higher priority to methods of relaxation and to noncompetitive forms of recreation.

4. To begin to learn methods of relaxation and centering as a key discipline in growing mentally and spiritually.

5. To be more aware of your internal conversation with your true self and to be more trusting of this interior way toward wisdom, love, and well-being.

6. To be open to some major changes in your life-style flowing out of your present commitments to be a growing person.

7. To gain confidence in your ability to tell the difference between genuine and false forms of spiritual growth.

These are ambitious expectations for a small book. I believe you can claim them for yourself, however, if you not only read the pages that follow but also participate fully in the exercises I offer along the way. The exercises I am including have been field-tested in personal practice in retreat settings for several years. Chapter 2 is built entirely around a new method of Bible study. It is designed to help you discover for yourself the level of readiness for being transformed to which you can commit yourself as you continue reading.

The following chapters will lead you step by step into the practice of the prayer-of-the-heart. The first lesson invites you into the experience of silence in which you may hear the still, small voice of God. The first lesson is the hardest. The remaining lessons explore the riches of being willing to be loved, of opening yourself to divine guidance, and of seeing clearly the differences between genuine and false forms of spiritual life.

As you finish the book you will have begun an exciting new chapter of your own life story. You will be ready to make good use of retreat experience as you journey on the inner way, and to share with others a new quality of life as transformation settles into life-style.

Chapter 2

Where to Begin

In my tradition two disciplines are at the heart of spiritual growth: Bible-reading and prayer. These are the disciplines I gave up as a young adult. I felt they had failed me. In the wake of the transforming moment that I shared with you in Chapter 1, I rediscovered both Bible-reading and prayer. Although at one level they are the same two disciplines, at another they now are radically different for me. The journey between discovery and rediscovery has made the difference.

In looking back, I begin to understand the story about a man who set out to climb a mountain. He left his base camp with visions of standing at the summit viewing a vast panorama and being beside himself with awe, peace, and joy. As he started out, a dense fog settled over the mountain. He struggled on, hardly able to see his feet in front of him, sometimes crawling on hands and knees. Finally, he reached what he thought was the peak of the mountain, and to his delight the fog began to lift. Breathlessly he strained for his first sight of the world below. As the sky cleared, he was stunned by what he saw. He was standing in his base camp—exactly where he was when he began the journey. At first he could not believe it, but gradually he sensed that everything around him, though familiar, was *different*. His having made the journey made the difference. Now he saw his world through new eyes—eyes filled with awe, peace, and joy. In the light of an inner transformation, the ordinary world itself was transformed.

A New Way of Bible Study

Something like this happened to my experience of Bible study and prayer. So I want now to invite you into a new way of Bible study with me. In the next chapter we will take a new look at prayer.

The whole fabric of transformation is woven together beautifully in the opening words of a section of practical guidance (at the end of profound theological writing) in Rom. 12:1–2:

> I appeal to you therefore, brethren, by the mercies of God, to present your bodies as a living sacrifice, holy and acceptable to God, which is your spiritual worship. Do not be conformed to this world but *be transformed* by the renewal of your mind, that you may prove what is the will of God, what is good and acceptable and perfect. (Italics added)

The method I want us to use in studying this passage is one I learned from Walter Wink. Wink is pioneering a way of Bible study which he presents in a book entitled *Transforming Bible Study* (Abingdon Press, 1980; see also Wink's first book on the subject, *The Bible in Human Transformation,* Fortress Press, 1973). The heartbeat of transforming Bible study is a rhythm between hard, critical study of a passage and relaxed, playful, yet honest response to the text. We respond in a dialogue process first and then in an activity. I will explain the method step by step as we go through it together.

The point of it, says Wink, is to free the text to speak to you in ways you are not accustomed to hearing. By responding spontaneously to questions about the passage, you allow the words of Scripture to enter you and you "begin the process of changing." Invest wholeheartedly in transforming Bible study and you contact "that lost dimension . . . where our own true face is known, and where what God is and what living is are one" (Wink, p. 43). Having used Wink's way of Bible study with good results for myself and others both in individual and small-group settings, I recommend your trying a form of it together, right here and now.

Phase I: Receiving the Text

First, make yourself comfortable, relaxed, and free from interruption.

Second, give yourself permission to take time for this experiment. Be as open as you can to self-discovery and to the possibility of hearing a word from God for you, yourself.

You may want to skip over the Bible study, and of course you may. I am making a strange offer, I realize. You expect to pick up a book and run through it without getting involved except in your thoughts. I am asking you, instead, to risk getting involved with yourself, and just possibly with the living God—right now in the reading of this book. (You may want to read quickly through the next several pages just to find out what all this is about and then decide whether to come back to this point and take the plunge. The exercise will take about an hour to complete.)

Third, deepen your relaxation by concentrating on your breathing for a few minutes. Breathe deeply—expanding your waist as you inhale and feeling the waist contract as you exhale.

Fourth, read Romans 12:1–2, aloud if possible. Repeat the reading several times, until the entire passage is nearly memorized.

Fifth, close the book, keeping your finger in the place, and repeat the passage aloud (or silently if you must). Open the book, check yourself, and, if you wish, reread it and again recite it to yourself, letting it become part of you.

Phase II. Dialoguing with the Text

Now, I will ask a series of questions based on my having studied the passage. As something comes to your mind in response to each question, write it on a piece of paper. My spontaneous responses are printed below the questions. Let the reading of my words flow across your awareness not as a guide for your thoughts but as improvisations on a theme. Proceed as if you were a jazz musician—developing the theme in your own way, allowing your thoughts to bounce off mine and to grow or fade away as they will.

Know that I am not seeking a right answer to the questions, I am only inviting you to let your responses flow freely as you open yourself to a time of discovery.

INSTRUCTIONS: Write whatever comes spontaneously to mind. Then return to the question and wait in a relaxed way for the next thing that comes to mind and write it down. Let your eyes fall on my words if you wish, but return again and again to the question, waiting for your own spontaneous responses and writing them down. When you feel that you have finished with the question, proceed to the next and so on through all seven questions.

QUESTION NO. 1: What are "the mercies of God" that have brought you to this moment, to considering an inner way of spiritual growth?

RESPONSES

A whole parade of alive, growing people—open to God!

A conspicuous failure when I was trying to fake it as a "spiritual" person.

A woman who understood what was happening in my spiritual journey, who encouraged and guided me at a fork in the road.

The Jewish readers in Rome to whom Paul was writing knew about animal sacrifice in Temple worship. Since the life of the animals was given up in death, their bodies were presented to God as dead sacrifices. Paul appeals to his readers to present their bodies "as a living sacrifice."

QUESTION NO. 2: How may I present my body as a living sacrifice?

RESPONSES

By being alive to my own true self.

By loving myself for God's sake—for the sake of loving and enjoying God and all the peoples, creatures, and worlds created by God's hand.

By taking time for myself—time for poetry, stories, and fishing, especially for fishing in season.

By regular, enjoyable exercise, sensible nutrition, and generally good health care of my body.

Paul sees a living sacrifice to be at the heart of "spiritual worship."

QUESTION NO. 3: What is spiritual worship in contrast to unspiritual worship?

RESPONSES

Being honest with myself before God!

It may mean being angry at God if that is how I honestly feel, whereas unspiritual worship may be denying my anger—being phony.

It is my life-style—attitudes, values, the works—not just going through the motions of worship, prayer, etc.

The old translation, "which is your reasonable service," is better translated, "which is your spiritual worship." The meaning is, allowing the prayer of the very Spirit of God who dwells in you to be prayed through you.

QUESTION NO. 4: Have you ever experienced something like this: an allowing of the Spirit within you to pray through you? If so, what state of mind are you in during these times?

RESPONSES

Relaxed concentration.

Oblivious of everything except the longing rising up from the deep places of the heart.

Falling asleep—trustingly.

Sometimes a pleasant blankness, yet a certain alertness. Other times, at my wits' end and spontaneously asking God's help—then experiencing deep bodily relaxation and an optimistic mood coming over me.

Moving toward personal application, Paul describes the results of spiritual worship and of the Spirit praying through you as not conforming yourself in mind and character to the pattern of the present age.

QUESTION NO. 5: What does it mean *for you* to be conforming yourself in mind and character to the pattern of the present age?

RESPONSES

Being concerned about what others will think.

Accepting uncritically the values of affluent living, of compliance with government in matters of national defense, especially nuclear weapons; also the values of "professionalism" when being professional prompts me to force the facts to fit my theories rather than to abandon familiar theories and follow the facts of my own experience wherever they may lead.

Next we have a passive imperative of the word *metamorphoō* from which we get the word "metamorphosis," meaning "any complete change in appearance, character, circumstances." The text says we are *to be transformed* by the renewal, or the remodeling, of our mind in order to correctly discern the will of God—what is the best and the most joyful, the most honorable or acceptable to God, and the most mature or most fully adult possible.

QUESTION NO. 6: What comes to mind when you think of the renewal, or the remodeling, of your mind in the direction of the best, most joyful, most honorable and acceptable to God, most mature and fully adult possible?

RESPONSES

Trusting my spontaneity.

Seeing the absurdities and humor in much of the "serious" talk I am part of.

Keeping silent more.

Being at home in my strengths as well as in my weaknesses.

Not working at being profound . . . or at "fixing" things.

Being who I am.

QUESTION NO. 7: If you were to be changed in a radical way, as from a caterpillar to a butterfly, and if the change were in the direction you have just described, what would be the first steps in that direction that you could take *today?*

RESPONSES

Relaxing ego control and trusting my spontaneity.

Praying from the heart to be more willing to be loved.

Recognizing fear as the face of evil.

I could claim a strong sense of satisfaction in offering my readers an original and potentially helpful exercise in spiritual growth.

Phase III. An Activity Embodying the Text

The final phase is the most important. It kicks up the most surprises, and God is in surprise more often than not. To stop with the mental activity of Phase II is to risk a miscarriage of the new life that has been conceived in you during the exercise.

You may want to avoid doing the activity in Phase III. Physical activities such as drawing, doing mime or role plays, working with clay, sand play, or paints may make you feel awkward and self-conscious. You do not like to "show yourself" in such ways. Yet the fact is that activities of the body often trigger understanding self and openings for the Spirit that come in no other way.

Read over the directions in the following paragraphs for an activity designed to help you embody the text you have studied. *Then face head on your inner resistance to doing it.* If you feel self-conscious or silly doing body movements, choose a less active exercise for now and try the body movements later when you feel more ready. If you decide not to do any of the activity options, give yourself at least one clear reason for not doing so. You might be surprised at what will come to mind if you complete the sentence:

> I choose not to do an activity embodying the text
> because . . .

Now if you are game to complete the Bible study, choose one of the following activity options.

Option No. 1: Drawing. Take a blank sheet of paper and several colored pens or crayons. Draw a vertical line dividing the sheet in half. In one half draw whatever you wish showing how you experience yourself when you are conforming yourself in mind and character to the pattern of this present age. Use colors to fit your feelings.

Then on the other half, draw whatever you wish showing how you experience yourself when you are being transformed by the renewal of your mind in the direction of the best, most joyful, most acceptable to God, and most mature. Again, use colors that fit your feelings about yourself.

Leave an inch or two of blank space across the bottom of the sheet of paper. When you have finished drawing, take a pen or a pencil and write a sentence or two under each drawing, putting your feelings about the drawing into words.

Finally, keep the drawing among your papers where you will see it from time to time. Every time you come across it, take a few minutes to befriend it—simply opening yourself to the impressions it makes on you.

Option No. 2: Posturing. Find a private place and walk about in it. Get a feel for being a body moving about. While doing this, choose a specific life situation in your real world. Let it be one in which you feel trapped in the need to conform yourself in mind and character to the pattern of this present age.

Then put yourself into a posture as if you were literally conformed—bound to another's pattern. Silently move your body into different postures until you find one in which you really feel tied up, paralyzed, or trapped.

Now let your posture become one of struggling not to be conformed. Feel the push and pull of the struggle.

Finally, posture yourself being transformed—being freed to be your true self, awake to God, free at last, at peace, yet fully alive. Let your experience be one in which you are being transformed by a force coming from beyond yourself, yet a force with which you cooperate fully.

When you complete the exercise, sit down at once and write a few sentences describing your feelings during each of the three stages: (1) being conformed, (2) struggling to be free, and (3) being transformed. Note any surprises you experienced during the activity and the meanings it has for you.

As in option No. 1, keep your written notes among your papers so that you will see them from time to time, and when you do, take a few minutes to reread them. Befriend the memory of the experience, and open yourself again to the meanings the experience had for you.

Option No. 3: Comparing Two Texts and Visualizing. Read Romans 6:1–11 and compare the two strong statements, 6:1–2, "Are we to continue in sin . . . ? By no means!" and 6:11, "you . . . must consider yourselves dead to sin and alive to God in Christ Jesus." Note that in this passage Paul assumes an experience of "renewal of the mind." "Oughts" and "should nots" have no place. Instead he says, you *cannot* live in sin, because the new life in Christ is spontaneous and free from duty—it is the only life possible, given the experience of "renewal." You have been transformed indeed. Then comes the final, summary statement: "So you also must consider yourselves dead to sin and alive to God in Christ Jesus" (Rom. 6:11).

Here, then, is a key to being transformed: to use your imagination to *visualize* yourself dead to sin and alive to God.

Now, sitting or lying down, relax and do some deep breathing. Choose an attitude, feeling, or behavior that is a troublesome part of your "old self"—something that conforms you in mind and character to the pattern of the present age.

Now, in your mind's eye see yourself indulging this part of your "old self" without any controls. Exaggerate the feelings and/or behaviors as much as you possibly can. See your old way as if it were a hot fire that you keep feeding and fanning.

Next, see the fire beginning to die down. You are out of fuel. The fire burns out and you feel yourself getting cold to the old part of you. Try to heat up the old way by blowing on the fire to make it flame up again. But without fuel the fire brightens a little, then dies down fast until the last sparks fade out and the old way is dead. Let yourself feel dead to your old way, sad at the loss of it, afraid of the emptiness, the coldness that sets in.

Then, see in your mind's eye a stirring in the cold ashes. See the ashes become like clay, being molded by invisible hands into a new you. Give yourself the body you would like to have, the weight, the face, the hair, the eyes. Then feel a strong wind blowing on you so that the new you comes alive. Feel powerful new energies move in your body. You are alive to your body as never before. You are alive to the new attitudes, feelings, and behaviors that you have most wanted to experience. You realize that the change is none other than God in you. You are alive to God in Christ Jesus, and the new ways just flow freely out of you.

Let yourself enjoy the sensations of being alive to God—joy, peace, and love. Let yourself be grateful for the hands that brought you to life out of the dead ashes of your old self and for the breath that blew across you making you alive to your own true self and also to God.

Gradually let go of the visualization and the sensations of being transformed.

You may wish to start a journal of your visualizations now. Enter the date and the part of your old self you visualized as dying and any surprises in visualizing yourself being transformed. Repeat the visualization frequently, every day if possible for several weeks, and not less than once a week for several months. Continue to record the different parts of your old self you visualize as dying and the discoveries you make as you "consider yourself dead to sin and alive to God in Christ Jesus."

Getting Down to Definitions

The time has come to define the key words I am writing about so as to make clear what I mean about "transformation," "the inner way," and "spiritual growth." I have invited you into a process of discovering your own next steps on the transformation journey before defining terms for a reason. Transformation is a picture word, not a measurement word. Growth stages are indicated by changes in external factors alone, but not so with transformations. Adolescence, for example, begins at puberty in specific bodily changes and ends in adulthood with a place in society. Without internal independence, transformation has not happened. To be transformed, therefore, is to be in touch with your inner world. So this is why I started with the Bible study designed to help you see where you are and where you are headed in your inner experience of your own true self.

Transformation

Transformation pictures a caterpillar spinning its cocoon, spending the winter asleep inside, then waking in the warmth of springtime, beating its way out of the cocoon, and discovering itself a butterfly. The caterpillar has been transformed. *Transformation is the emergence of new forms and functions in which discontinuity with the old is marked.* Change occurs in transformations, but change also occurs without transformations. Change may be an alteration of forms and functions without discontinuity with the old. I call this *formation.* The difference between formation and transformation is important to understand. To risk being transformed is to risk major change, letting go of old ways of being within yourself. *Formation* is a process of shaping something or someone. It refers here to the way you arrange things in your life as it is today. *Transformation* means being in a different place or condition, in a place beyond the old place.

You may picture this, applied to growing up and growing older, as a ten-story building. (Ken Wilber develops the image in *The Atman Project: A Transpersonal View of Human Development,* p. 40; Theosophical Publishing House, 1980.) Within each level, the work of *formation* goes on. Movement between levels is *transformation.* A lot of change may go on within any given level of the building: furnishings are brought in, moved about, tried this way and that. Many styles of interior decoration may be tried. But continuity prevails because the basic structure of the building remains unchanged. For example, let us say that the third floor is the developmental level of preschool children. A child may develop new food preferences every few weeks or become very particular about clothing choices, but these changes are contained within a fixed structure which Wilber calls The Image-Body Self (Wilber, p. 19). Within this third-floor structure, magical thinking prevails for all children. Wish fulfillment, anxiety reduction, safety and security needs are the rule. Time sense is the present—just here and now. Self awareness centers in body image.

Then comes a *transformation*. The child finds the stairwell, gets on it and discovers it is an escalator that dumps people off on the fourth floor (or, if in regression, back down to the second floor). Old formations break up; chaos, pain, and crisis prevail for a while. Once on the fourth floor, however, the process of formation recurs, but this time in a new structure. The child now explores a new self—a self that is now verbal and membership-oriented. Time begins to be formed into past and future as well as present (thanks to the learning of tenses as part of new verbal skills); the fourth floor contains the roots of willpower, autonomous choice and belongingness, durable likes and dislikes, and mythical thinking. (Wilber, p. 28.)

Spiritual Growth

Every time you find the stairwell and are lifted to the next level, a *transformation* occurs and the old *formations* are transcended. If you visualize God as owner, architect, builder, chief occupant, and host of the entire building, you see that all growth from stage to stage extends your knowledge and enjoyment of God. As you advance from one level to another, you gain the ability to help your host maintain and improve the building. Best of all, as your awareness of the generosity of your host grows, especially as you discover the penthouse and at times enjoy the undivided presence of your host, your love and devotion take a quantum leap forward. To your surprise and delight, each transformation has awakened you to higher and higher levels of awareness, of purpose, and of the will to be at one with your host.

Spiritual growth, then, is a process of transformation toward being at one with God. Every experience of getting yourself together, every move toward your true self, whether resolving conflicts of body and mind or turning enemies into friends or being lifted to a higher level of consciousness, is an experience of God, and a foretaste of perfect at-oneness with God.

An Inner Way

What remains is to speak of the inner way. An inner way implies an outer way, and both ways are essential in spiritual growth. There is a time to travel the outer way and a time for the inner way. Before moving ahead on the journey that is before you in this book, you need to know the difference. You need also to decide whether the time is at hand for taking the inner way toward the next transformation on your spiritual journey.

Wilber offers a useful comment on the image of life as a circle. Beginning with birth at the bottom center of the circle and moving up the left side to the midpoint at the top, the line forms an "outward arc." Coming down the right side, it is an "inward arc." (Wilber, pp. 4–5.) Actually by the time a person enters puberty, the outward arc begins to level off toward the inward arc. The outward arc traces growth from a "prepersonal" (preverbal and subconscious) state to a highly developed state of personhood. This is as far as most psychologies go today in mapping the spiritual journey. But there is more, much more.

The inward arc traces growth from personal to transpersonal states of consciousness (transverbal and superconscious).

Artists, musicians, poets, storytellers, seers, and saints are acquainted with transpersonal experience. You travel the inward arc on the inner way, from self-consciousness to self-surrender. As the development of rational thinking is a vast improvement over the prerational mental activities of an infant, so the development of intuition, illumination, bliss, love-bondedness, and being at one with God, is a vast improvement over depending only on rational ways of knowing. Traveling an inner way along the inward arc, you do not lose the skills of the outer way. Self-consciousness is not lost; it is expanded to include God-consciousness. Rationality is not lost, it is displaced from the center, becoming an ally rather than an enemy of intuition, imagination, and inspiration—the superconscious ways of knowing.

The inner way, then, is a way of life shaped by a conscious desire to be at one with God and formed around a core of disciplines that enable you to transcend self-consciousness and rational ways of knowing in order to develop superconscious knowing and loving and thus to experience the Presence of God directly. In so doing, you heighten greatly your capacity to glorify God and to enjoy him, forever!

Now comes a "go" or "no-go" decision. Only you can decide whether you desire to be at one with God enough to explore the core disciplines of an inner way of spiritual growth. If your answer is yes, you will want to move on into the remaining chapters of the book. If no, you will do well to put the book aside for another day. For as surely as you live and grow, the time will come when you will be ready to travel the inner way. That readiness must be interior and genuine, however. To start on the inner way without a longing love for God is to set out on an impossible journey. To be ready is to be setting foot already on the escalator up to the next level.

Chapter 3

The First Lesson Is the Hardest

Now that you have discovered in yourself a longing for spiritual growth you are ready for the first lesson. The object of the first lesson is twofold: to experience a new way of being and a new way of knowing. The new way of being is sometimes called *not-doing* and the new way of knowing is called *not-knowing*. Not-doing is something you do and not-knowing is a way of knowledge. You are not to become purely passive or to stop thinking. Not-doing is a form of passive activity and not-knowing is a way toward intuitive wisdom.

Visualize the first lesson as learning to shift from head to heart. Your goal is to move toward wholeheartedness—listening to God with a longing for God. In this sense you shift from the work of the head, which is thinking about and analyzing, to the activity of the heart, which is longing love. But this is the focus of the second lesson in Chapter 4. The first lesson is learning to relax your need *to do* and *to know* in the usual sense of doing a task and getting information or solving problems. You learn, instead, *to be still* in body and in mind, *to wait* on the Lord, *to listen* to the still, small voice within, and simply *to be present*—present to your body, to your own true self and to God.

Not-Doing

You do not-doing by relaxing and drawing your attention into your body. It is just that simple. In fact, both parts of the first lesson are so simple that most people find it the hardest lesson of all.

Most of us are like the woman who decided she would like to learn to play the flute. Going to a teacher, she asked how much the lessons would cost.

"Ten gold pieces for the first lesson," said the teacher. "One gold piece for every lesson thereafter."

She thought for a while and then replied: "Good. I shall begin with the second lesson."

I can promise you one reward for not skipping the not-doing lesson: you will learn to enjoy silence and to relax. In fact, you will develop the ability to relax anytime and anywhere you wish. You will welcome silence and seek it. It will be like coming home. You will look forward to the times of being nowhere, not-doing and not-knowing.

Guides You Can Trust

If I were with you in person, I would invite you right now to put the book down and allow me to direct you in some simple exercises that would create for you an experience of not-doing. Instead, I will introduce you to some guides you can trust to open the door into relaxation, silence, and inner ways of spiritual growth.

First, I commend to you the book that served me well on the first stage of the journey: Lawrence LeShan, *How to Meditate: A Guide to Self-Discovery* (Little, Brown & Co., 1974; Bantam Books, 1975). LeShan is a psychologist whose awakening to the spiritual journey was aided by the pastoral care specialist and Christian mystic, Edgar Jackson. *How to Meditate* is a noncultic introduction to meditation, describing a wide range of exercises you can use as disciplines of spiritual growth and inner transformation.

A down-to-earth book on meditation is Harry Meserve's *The Practical Meditator* (Human Sciences Press, 1981). Meserve adds to the "how to" section a fine collection of "Sentences to Live With" and "Paragraphs to Ponder." His years as a worship leader yield a full harvest in these pages.

For the person who tends to make work of everything—including relaxation—I recommend Gerald May's *The Open Way: A Meditation Handbook* (Paulist Press, 1977). May is a psychiatrist and a spiritual director. He is direct, matter-of-fact, able to laugh at himself, and able to make you want to relax your need to make a big deal out of meditation and spiritual awareness.

A book I turn to often now is Anthony de Mello, S.J., *Sadhana: A Way to God, Christian Exercises in Eastern Form* (1978; Institute of Jesuit Sources, Fusz Memorial, St. Louis University, 3700 W. Pine Blvd., St. Louis, Mo. 63108). De Mello is director of the Sadhana Institute of Pastoral Counseling in Poona, India, where retreat masters and spiritual directors receive training. Sadhana leads you into silence and body awareness; then into centering and contemplation.

I shall now try to sell you on paying the price—all ten gold coins—required for the first lesson. The rest of the chapter states the case for beginning to practice meditation as the first lesson on the inner way of being transformed.

Sitting Still in Silence and Breathing

You begin meditation exercises by sitting for a few minutes in silence. Next you repeat the experience of silence, with your mind centered on your breathing. What could be more simple or more basic than sitting still and breathing? When you do this for the first time, however, you discover some things in the silence that surprise you.

You may be surprised by how unfamiliar silence feels. Try to concentrate at one point, such as your breathing, and you see how busy the mind is: flitting from this to that, stirring up a variety of feelings, fantasies, and daydreams—all in the space of just a few minutes. Perhaps as you get near the edge of silence, you will panic and withdraw. Silence can be scary, and that too may be a surprise.

When you sense your mind wandering or dozing off, and your body twitching and itching, you are on the way to experiencing silence as a revelation. *For of all the revelations of silence, the central one is to reveal you to your self.* In silence you discover not only your mind's noise and your body's antics but also your true self in the act of observing your mind and body. You build on this awareness in the exercises of the first lesson. As you continue with the centering exercises, you make friends with your true, inner self, and you grow to like your true self more and more.

Then, one day you realize that God is meeting you in your centered self. The silence is filled with the sound of God's still, small voice. An old proverb puts it well:

> For one who enters the woods noisily, the woods
> are silent. For one who enters the woods silently,
> the woods are filled with sound.

As a bird-watcher, I can talk without scattering the birds, so long as I do so softly, but I must be still in body. Becoming still in body is step two in making contact with your true self and hearing the still, small voice of God.

From Your Head to Your Heart

As you do not-doing, you stretch your ability to be still in body. This comes more easily than you think if you start small—sitting just a few minutes at a time—and gradually increase the time over several months. More difficult, however, is not-doing in your mind. Your mind races even though the body is perfectly still; it shouts within, no matter how deep the silence may be without. So a basic goal is to shift your attention from your head to your heart. You do this by relaxing and drawing your attention into your body. Then, lo and behold, by body awareness, by waking to the sensations of your body, you make progress toward being with God.

What a surprise! Many people are reared to dislike their body sensations. They deaden their sensory awareness and think of bodily needs as the enemy of spiritual growth. I want to stand these notions on their head. Instead of denying bodily sensations, fearing and fighting them, welcome them. Pay attention to them, observe and explore them, and you find that waking to your body becomes the entrance into the sanctuary of the Divine Presence.

Early Christians understood the primacy of the body. Gregory of Nyssa (A.D. 335–395), one of the chief architects of Christian spirituality in ancient times, describes the inner way of spiritual growth as an endless ascent. You begin in the awakening of longing love for God. The second stage is catharsis, or purification. Only then do you enter the third stage of illumination and move on to the fourth stage of being at one with God. Notice that the body metaphor of catharsis, or purification, comes prior to the mental image of illumination. Not only metaphorically but also descriptively, the stage of purification requires, first of all, attention to the body. For Gregory the steps in purification are: (1) transcending passions, (2) transcending moralism and legalism, (3) transcending materialism, and (4) transcending rationalism. Transcending your passions comes first. This requires you to acknowledge your passions, to enter into and move through your passions, and thus, in effect, to enter the cathedral of the soul through the body en route to the heart.

The body, says the apostle Paul, "is a temple of the Holy Spirit within you, which you have from God. You are not your own; you were bought with a price. So glorify God in your body" (I Cor. 6:19–20). Enter the prayer-of-the-heart through body awareness and you understand Paul's plea to glorify God in your body. You actually experience the body as a temple of the Holy Spirit. You discover in your body the inner reality of the Spirit's Presence and the nourishment of divine energy. You are freed from the need to pretend in the life of prayer. You come to love your body—for God's sake! You respect your body's needs, take care for its feeding and its exercise, its rest and recreation, its postures and its appearance. And you do so, not out of pride or anxieties about good health, but out of love and admiration for the temple of the Holy Spirit that it is, and for the joy of glorifying God in the inner, silent places of body awareness.

Anthony de Mello tells of a friend who sought instruction in the art of prayer. His teacher said to him, "Concentrate on your breathing."

After five minutes the friend was ready for further instruction. His teacher then said: *"The air you breathe is God. You are breathing God in and out. Become aware of that, and stay with that awareness."*

De Mello reported that his friend followed these instructions day after day, discovering that prayer became as simple a matter as breathing in and out. To his surprise, he experienced more satisfaction from this form of prayer than he had found in the many hours devoted to mental prayer over a period of many years. (De Mello, pp. 3–4.)

Yes, prayer can be as simple as breathing. I hope you will open yourself both to your breathing and to all your body sensations as signals of the Holy Spirit within you. In doing so, you are praying not only with your head but also with your heart. You move away from thinking about God into being present to God, and, in the experience of presence, you find yourself loving God with a whole heart.

Body and Sensory Awareness

The next phase of your training in not-doing is to increase your body and sensory awareness. Progressive muscle relaxation makes this lesson easy and rewarding.

The Jacobson Method of Progressive Relaxation was developed early in this century by the physician L. E. Jacobson. You simply pay attention to all the muscle systems of the body in succession—progressing from the head to the toes or vice versa. You scan the body, giving tension areas simple, loving awareness, and then let each muscle system drop into deep relaxation as you move on. It may be done also by intentionally tensing a muscle system to a point of maximum tightness, then letting go and moving on to the next area, repeating the rhythm of tensing and letting go as you progress throughout the body.

Begin in a comfortable posture, feet flat on the floor, buttocks back in the chair, back straight but not rigid, head balanced on the spine like a ball atop a pole.

Let your eyes gently close.

Let all your muscles loosen and relax. Let your body weight sink down fully onto the surface on which you are sitting.

Then focus your awareness on the bottom of your feet—toes, arch, heel—becoming aware of the contact of your feet with the floor. If you sense any tension sensations, simply hold that area of the body in awareness, opening yourself to the sensations, exploring them, being present to them. You are allowing your body to make claims on your attention. You are being present to the body part that is signaling tension—awake to it, lovingly aware.

Now draw your attention up to the ankles, then the calves. Once again be aware of any tension signals—twitching, throbbing, or pain. Gently hold the sensations in your awareness—you are giving your body a kind of mental massage. Then let go, allowing that muscle system to drop into deep relaxation, to be completely at rest, and move on to the next area of the body.

Move your attention upward to the knees, the thighs, the buttocks. Allow the body openings in the pelvic region to relax. Be aware of your body's contact with the chair. Let all your weight down onto the chair and the floor.

Now focus on your diaphragm. Let your breathing be deep, diaphragmatic, and regular.

Shift your attention to the base of the spine and move progressively upward—disc by disc—being aware of any burning or pain sensations as you go, and, again, holding all such signals in awareness. Do not be in a hurry. You are simply being good to your body, being caring, lovingly aware.

As you reach the top of the spine, shift awareness to the shoulder blades, rotating them a bit if they are tight or tension-filled, then let them be.

Become aware of your chest area. Then go to the shoulders, upper arms, elbows, lower arms, and hands. You may wish to twitch each finger in turn, letting each one go completely limp and at rest as you move along.

As you progress, draw your consciousness up and out of the lower body toward your head. Allow your body to be inert. You may lose conscious contact with your body almost altogether.

Focus next on your neck. Check to see that your head has not dropped onto your chest, nor been thrown back with the chin high. Let the head be balanced on the neck like a ball atop a pole. Be aware of your swallowing and your breath passing easily through the neck.

Shift your attention to the mouth. Let the lower jaw drop free, your tongue lie limp in the mouth. You may become aware of tension flowing out of the joint of the jaw.

Next focus on your nose, on the sensations of the air flowing in and out.

Move your attention to the eyes. Become aware of any burning sensations or fatigue in the eyes and hold them gently in awareness. If your eyelids are tightly closed, open them just enough to receive a sliver of light through the eyelashes and let them close again ever so lightly.

Now move your awareness to your ears. Open yourself to all the sounds around you. Concentrate intently on hearing more and more subtle sounds. Do not analyze or hold on to the sounds, simply allow them to flow through your awareness.

And now, center your attention on your scalp. Allow the tiny muscles of the scalp and forehead to relax. Become aware of the folds of the skin smoothing out—down the forehead, down toward the ears. As the scalp relaxes, it is as if breathing space opens up around the root of each hair.

Know now that you are deeply relaxed. Your body energy is flowing freely from the top of your head to the tip of your toes. Allow yourself to enjoy the sensations of well-being that flow through your body. Congratulate yourself for taking good care of your body, making friends with it, listening to it, and honoring it as the sanctuary of the Holy Spirit.

And now, you may wish to open yourself to the deepest longing of your heart. Allow it to come into consciousness and release it to God in a single word or phrase. It is the prayer-of-your-heart. Know that the Spirit makes intercession with our spirits with groanings that cannot be uttered (Rom. 8:26). So if no words come into awareness, simply be open to your true self, allowing the Holy Spirit to pray for you and through you.

As you are ready, taking the time you need, let go of the relaxation exercise and of your interior prayer. Prepare yourself to return to the world of ordinary awareness. Stretch your toes and your fingers. Take a deep breath and open your eyes.

You may be wondering now what connection can be found between sensuous experiences and spirituality. To be sure, sensory awareness is not necessarily spiritual awareness, but it may prepare the way for the coming of the Spirit. The connection is preparation for not-knowing.

Not-Knowing

One way to see the connection is to look at the several states of consciousness related to levels of relaxation and centeredness. A breakthrough in research came with development of encephalographic readings (EEG). Four states of consciousness are linked with levels of EEG activity. On a scale from zero to 26 hertz (Hz) per second, the EEG measures frequency and intensity of brain wave activity. Going from high to low, the four ranges are as follows:

Beta (26 to 12 Hz)
When the EEG records brain activity in the Beta range, you are in an ordinary, waking state of consciousness, or in a state

of focused attention. You do rational thinking, decision-making, conversation, and the like. Beta is the range of knowing in contrast to not-knowing.

Alpha (12 to 8 Hz)

Alpha is a state of defocused attention. You experience a peaceful, pleasant blankness. The rational activity of the brain is slowing down and fading out. Some people are uncomfortable with the empty blankness of the Alpha state, but others welcome it.

Given a positive attitude toward the Alpha state, you allow it to prepare you for insights, problem-solving, and creativity. Alpha is the range in which meditation begins to happen. When you combine relaxation with a centering exercise, your brain wave activity slows in frequency and intensity and drops from the Beta into the Alpha range. In Alpha, you enter the realm of not-knowing.

Theta (8 to 4 Hz)

Theta is a twilight zone of half-consciousness or reverie. Dreamlike images flow through your awareness when you are in this range. Most of your experiencing is lost to consciousness, however. Experienced meditators may drop down into Theta and then hover on the boundary between Alpha and Theta. In this process, you may do what is called Active Imagination. Dreamlike images are lifted into consciousness. You then dialogue with the images. You direct the "dream," as it were, going down into Theta and allowing the "dream" to flow; then rising up to the boundary of Alpha, dialoguing and directing the process; then dropping down again into Theta; and so on. Useful discoveries often come to light in this mode of not-knowing.

Delta (4 to 0 Hz)

Delta is sleeping consciousness. Surprisingly, the quality of mental refreshment is not as good in Delta as in Alpha and Theta. You are more refreshed in a twenty-minute meditation, for example, than in a twenty-minute nap.

Herbert Benson, a Harvard professor of medicine, reports in his best-seller, *The Relaxation Response* (William Morrow & Co., 1975; Avon Books, 1976), that helpful changes in blood pressure, heart rate, and many other autonomic nervous system functions happen in meditation (i.e., in Alpha and Theta) but do not occur as often when the same amount of time is spent in relaxation alone or in sleeping (i.e., Beta or Delta). Meditation and sleeping are not in any way interchangeable. Both are needed for good health, of course.

All of this may seem foreign to your experience of daily living. The fact is, however, that you experience all four states of consciousness at least twice in every twenty-four-hour cycle of your lives. Falling asleep, you pass from the waking state of Beta into Alpha as you lose interest in the world beyond your bed. You drop on down into Theta, in which you are not yet asleep but no longer fully awake, and then into Delta. During sleep you come up into Theta in a rhythmic pattern of dreaming. Upon waking you come first into Theta, in which you are not awake, yet no longer asleep. You may waken in a dream and be confused as to which is real—the dream or the external world of which you are now dimly aware. Reality-testing slowly returns as you come on up through Alpha into Beta. Your energy, then, is reinvested in the world of ordinary consciousness and everyday tasks.

These mid-range states of not-knowing—i.e., Alpha and Theta—happen often in the midst of daily duties as well as around the edges of sleep. Turnpike driving may produce "highway hypnosis," a trancelike state (probably in the Alpha-

Theta range) in which you drive for miles at high speeds, passing many exits with no conscious awareness at all. A teenager entranced with stereophonic music may be literally in a trance state (in the Alpha-Theta range). Down at police headquarters a victim of the third degree may be driven systematically into an altered state of consciousness as is the penitent at the mourners' bench during a revival meeting. Reading trances occur at poetry-reading clubs, and similar states of Alpha-Theta consciousness delight the devotees of health spas as members go from vigorous exercise to sitting in whirlpool baths and steam saunas. Awarenesses take place in all of these ways that go beyond ordinary thinking. Call them insights, "aha" moments, confessions, revelations, or conversions, they are the many faces of not-knowing.

From Left-Brain to Right-Brain

Studies of bimodal consciousness suggest that as you drop into the Alpha state, the brain switches from mainly rational to intuitive ways of knowing or from ordinary knowing to not-knowing. While all the evidence is not in, it appears that for some people the left hemisphere of the brain controls rational ways of knowing, while the right hemisphere does intuitive and mystic knowing. Could it be that the brain is built to function as well in mystical as in rational ways of knowing? A great deal of evidence points in that direction. It is also clear that by deciding to relax and concentrate in a centering exercise, you can at any time tap into the intuitive powers of the mind and activate alternate states of consciousness.

I well remember a number of years ago sharing these research findings with a friend. I spoke excitedly as if I had hold of a revolutionary idea. When I finished, there was a long pause. He then looked at me and, with a perfectly sincere tone, said, "So?"

I was stunned. How, I wondered, could he not have grasped the impact of these findings for himself and for the religious life? I wondered how I failed to make clear its meanings. What was I taking for granted that needed to be spelled out? As time went on, I realized that he had little appetite at that time for the life of the Spirit. What I overlooked in the telling was that findings about alternate states of consciousness and intuitive ways of not-knowing do not *necessarily* inform the spiritual life. Thus, unless you are actively seeking to understand and increase your awareness of the spiritual realm, the proper response is a puzzled, "So?" or a cynical, "So what?"

Fishing and Spirituality

Not long after, while on a fishing trip, I came up with an analogy that may answer the question, "So what?" A "structure" fisher knows that you find fish only in a tiny percentage of a lake's area. The fish are confined to certain roadways along which they travel in search of food and shelter. You can see what I mean if you visualize a lake as a huge bathtub. Pull the plug, drain the water, and visualize the structures on the bottom of the lake. There are old streambeds that provide natural travel routes for the fish. Old roadways provide easy and safe access from deep to shallow water for feeding. Terraced drop-offs with objects on them like brush or rock piles provide safe shelter as fish move up from their deepwater sanctuaries into the shallows to feed. An experienced fisher does not waste time in trial-and-error fishing all over the lake. Instead, the wise fisher visualizes the bottom structures of the lake and casts at those points where the likelihood of meeting fish is greatest.

A wise seeker after God does not rely on trial and error either. Neither do you trust completely the folklore you have heard from oldtimers in years past. You pay attention to the structures of the Spirit built into the human body and brain. Doing so increases the likelihood that you will make contact with the Life that moves in the depths of the universe.

So? So, learn the techniques of relaxation and centering, of moving at will into the Alpha and Theta states of consciousness, of using the right hemisphere of the brain—your intuitive, nonverbal, timeless, and mystic mode of not-knowing. In so doing, you increase the likelihood of being grasped by the living God, who comes out of the depths to find those who are open and ready for contact.

A spiritual guide once received a university professor who came seeking spiritual direction. In serving tea, he poured his visitor's cup full, and then kept pouring. The professor watched the overflow until he could no longer stand it.

"It is overfull," cried the professor. "No more will go in!"

"Like this cup," the spiritual guide said, "you are full of your opinions and speculations. How can I show you the spiritual way unless you first empty your cup?"

Here was one who understood the structures of the Spirit. The point of this chapter—the first and hardest lesson—is that progress on the path of spiritual growth requires us to shift attention from our heads to our hearts. We do so by not-doing and not-knowing. Relaxation combined with centering in body and sensory awareness is a reliable structure for doing not-doing and for gaining the knowledge of not-knowing.

How you get into your heart and what it means to pray with the mind in the heart with longing love is the subject of the second lesson—and the following chapter.

Chapter 4

The Sharp Dart
of Longing Love

This chapter is about being at one with God: it is about interior prayer, about longing love, about the Presence, and about the mind being in the heart. The metaphor of the heart means to love. It means also to live. Loving and living are joined, for in loving you are most fully alive and in living the life of the Spirit you are awake to a longing love for God.

The Cloud of Unknowing

One of the gems of Christian spirituality is the anonymous fourteenth-century work called *The Cloud of Unknowing*. My favorite passage contains the phrase that I have used for the title of this chapter: "the sharp dart of longing love." The author was probably an English monk who was familiar with an ancient tradition of Christian spirituality.

"Your whole life," he writes, "must be one of longing." The longing is put in your hearts by God with your consent. "God is ready when you are," he adds, "and is waiting for you." Unhappily, when you set out on the journey of longing love, you find only darkness—"as it were a cloud of unknowing." (*The Cloud of Unknowing*, tr. Clifton Wolters; Penguin

Books, 1961. This and following quotations come from pp. 52–61.)

Do what you will, this cloud remains between you and God, and stops you "both from seeing him in the clear light of rational understanding, and from experiencing his loving sweetness."

You, then, are urged to wait patiently in the darkness as long as necessary, but to go on longing after God. For, you are told, "if you are to feel him or to see him in this life, it must always be in this cloud, in this darkness." The crux of the matter comes next: God is unknowable to the intellect, but "not to our love."

The power of loving works through "a cloud of forgetting." The passage that follows reads like a modern guidebook on meditation. You are advised to put aside everything you can think, including devotional thoughts about God's kindness and worth. All thinking is to be covered in "a cloud of forgetting." Then comes the purple passage that for me goes to the heart of interior prayer:

> And you are to step over it [the cloud of forget-ting] resolutely and eagerly, with a devout and kindling love, and try to penetrate that darkness above you. *Strike that thick cloud of unknowing with the sharp dart of longing love,* and on no account whatever think of giving up. (Italics add-ed)

Do you feel the energy in this passage? Do you sense the will to stick to it, the longing, the confidence that God may be met, the trust in the power of love? Yet the active power of this longing works in a state of passivity—in bodily relaxation and a centered mind. Here, then, is the first of many logical contradictions in the life of interior prayer. When you shift your attention from head to heart, you are in for many surprises. The prayer-of-the-heart occurs in a state of active passivity or of passive activity. Both are essential. With passivity alone, you go into a trancelike state. You are blissful but not necessarily awake to God. With activity alone, you have only mental prayer. Your thoughts may be profound, but they are not able to transform you.

The Prayer-of-the-Heart

Prayer is of three kinds: vocal, mental, and interior or prayer-of-the-heart. In public worship vocal prayer is usually done by a professional, that is, by an ordained clergyperson. Public prayers are usually full of decorated sentences addressed to God, offering cues for the mental prayers of the congregation. Unfortunately the only models most people ever have for praying are vocal prayers.

Mental prayers remain, for many, exercises in thinking rather than experiences of relating to God. They are filled with words, too, subvocalized words. The words may be "empty phrases," which Jesus criticized in the prayers of the Pharisees (Matt. 6:7). They may, of course, be sincere. Have you noticed that the more sincere you are in mental prayer, the fewer words you use? Sincerity in prayer moves you toward letting go the forms of prayer in favor of simple speech and few words uttered wholeheartedly. Thus you stumble upon the reality of the prayer-of-the-heart.

The prayer-of-the-heart is not thinking about God. It is wholeheartedly longing for God. From time to time it is experiencing the Presence of God. Being lifted out of yourself by a powerful spiritual force is the way some people speak of the experience. Being bathed in love, joy, and peace; enveloped in light, enlightened by truth, and awakened to your own true self—these are some of the images people use to try to tell what happens in prayer when the mind is in the heart. (For a beautifully written study of the prayer-of-the-heart in the earliest Christian writings, see Henri Nouwen, *The Way of the Heart: Desert Spirituality and Contemporary Ministry;* Seabury Press, 1981.)

You see why relaxation and centering are essential aspects of interior prayer. The disciplines of the first lesson move you away from merely thinking about God into a state of not-doing and not-knowing, which is preparation for directly experiencing God. Interior prayer is being-in-relation with God. It is meeting God from the bottom of your heart rather than off the top of your head.

I label the acts in the drama of my spiritual journey by three injunctions:

> Act I: To Pray
> Act II: Not to Pray
> Act III: To Not-Pray

In my youth I learned mental prayer (Act I: To Pray). Later, as I have told, I decided to do only vocal or ritual prayer but not to pray mentally in private devotions (Act II: Not to Pray). A decade ago, in waking to the Presence and to my own true self, I found, also, the treasure of not-praying (Act III: To Not-Pray). To not-pray is not a negation of prayer. It is rather the passive activity that has been called, from the earliest Christian writings, the prayer-of-the-heart.

There is a well-known story in India of a girl crossing a place where a Holy Man is saying his prayers. The law is that no one shall cross a person who is praying. To cross means to allow your shadow to move across the person at prayer.

When the girl returns, she crosses the Holy Man again. "How insolent!" the man shouts. "Do you not know what you have done?"

"What did I do?" asks the girl. And the man tells her that she has crossed him while he was praying.

"I did not mean any harm," says the girl. "But tell me, what do you mean by praying?"

"For me, prayer is thinking of God," says the man.

"Oh," she says, "I was going to see my young man, and I was thinking of him, and I did not see you. But if you were thinking of God, how did you see me?" (*Tales Told by Hazrat Ināyat Khan,* p. 1; Sufi Order Publications, 1980.)

Here, in the story, is the clue to the prayer-of-the-heart. The Holy Man is doing mental prayer—thinking about God. But the young lady is wholeheartedly present to her young man even though physically separated from him. This is the reality of what it means to not-pray or to pray with the mind in the heart.

The In-Love Analogy

The story says something else as well. Interior prayer is being in love with God. When you are in love and thinking of your loved one, you are right there with your beloved. You are blind and deaf to everyone and everything else. You take delight in every moment that you can steal your attention away from your daily work to be with your loved one—in your heart. In such moments your beloved is fully present to you. Unknown to you, you are also being transformed into the likeness of the other. You are thinking the same thoughts, desiring the same things, seeing things from the same point of view. Slowly but surely, you are being changed from one degree of likeness to another. Is it any wonder that the apostle Paul speaks of the spiritual journey as our beholding with unveiled face the glory of the Lord, and "being changed into his likeness from one degree of glory to another; for this comes from the Lord who is the Spirit" (II Cor. 3:18)?

Being in love can be scary, too. The transforming power of a love relationship threatens you with inner as well as outer change. The intimacy that warms and nourishes also frightens. Myron Madden says that most of us have a "God phobia." We want to keep our distance if possible. Madden, who is a hospital chaplain, tells with lilt and humor of walking into a group of nurses who were meeting in a room next to the hospital chapel and telling them that as he came through the chapel he had a most unusual experience. He was met by God in physical form—as real as George Burns in the movie *"Oh, God!"* God said for him to tell the nurses that he would be in the chapel for a while and any nurse who would like to come in and talk to him about anything would be welcome. When asked how many would like to believe that this was true and, if it were, would be willing to take God up on his offer, not one nurse volunteered to go. Madden then asked how many would go if it were Jesus instead of God. Two or three were willing to risk meeting Jesus. I have played the same game with several groups of seminary students, ministers, and laity in church groups—*with the very same results!* As we talk about it, many people—clergy included—admit to something like a God phobia.

Raise a window shade on a dark night just as lightning flashes across the landscape and you will close your eyes and quickly draw the shade to protect yourself from the brightness. So it is, says St. Symeon, the tenth-century mystic, with a person who is enclosed in the realm of ordinary reality. One peep outside through the window of interior prayer and you are overwhelmed by the radiance of the Holy Spirit within. Afraid of the Presence of the living God, you draw back into the safety of your house of everyday awareness. (Kenneth Leech, *True Prayer: An Invitation to Christian Spirituality,* p. 3; Harper & Row, 1981.)

The in-love analogy points not only to the conflict between approaching and avoiding the Presence of our divine lover, but also to some specific behaviors that begin to happen on venturing into the prayer-of-the-heart.

A Sparsity of Words

One such behavior is reducing the number of words you use in prayer. Often you will utter only a single word or phrase. The prayer process flows from relaxation into a centering meditation. Then as you open yourself to the deepest longings of your heart, a single word or phrase leaps up. You release it to God. It is the prayer of your heart. You have a sense of absolute certitude about it. It is carried on the wings of the Spirit to God, where you are heard, received, and loved in unconditional love. No other words are needed except perhaps another impulse of gratitude and thanksgiving. Sometimes an impulse defies words altogether—leaping wordlessly to God. Such moments match the experience of the apostle Paul when he says, "The Spirit helps us in our weakness; for we do not know how to pray as we ought, but the Spirit himself intercedes for us with sighs too deep for words" (Rom. 8:26).

You can get some feel for the richness of this experience of prayer by calling to mind an intimate moment with a person you dearly love. In the moment you are now remembering, what use did you make of words? I suspect that you used few, if any. You may have said it all in the meeting of your eyes, or in reaching out a hand and touching or embracing your loved one. If you used words at all, you may have said, "I'm here," or "I came as soon as I heard," or "I love you." If you were the needy one, you may have said, "Don't leave me!" or "I need you!" or "Help me, please!" So it is in praying with the mind in the heart. Your utterances may be as sparse as a cry for help, a vow of devotion, or a plea, "Come, Holy Spirit, come!" You may, of course, ask guidance on specific problems or commit yourself in love for another. But of petitions and intercessions, I shall speak a bit farther on.

More than anything else, the prayer-of-the-heart is an experience of glorifying and enjoying God. To pray with the mind in the heart is to be "orthodox." Orthodoxy does not literally mean "right belief," as defined in a dictionary, but "right glory"! In both the Greek and the Latin stems, *doxa* means glory or praise, as in "doxology." Moments of genuine *doxa* are expressed best in art, in song, in poetry, and in the prayer-of-the-heart. In the next several pages I shall hold interior prayer up to the light, turn it slowly as if it were a diamond, and let the *doxa* within it shine through. Finding words to tell about any experience of the heart is difficult, and more so with religious experience. I am driven to poetry for help and to a poem, called "A Song," by one who wants to remain anonymous. The poet is traveling the inner way of spiritual growth and is striking the cloud of unknowing with the sharp dart of longing love.

Wisdom in Affection

"A Song" begins:

> You have loved me with an everlasting love.
> *So much wisdom is in that affection.* (Italics added)

And so much spiritual wisdom is in the words: wisdom in affection! You praise God best as longing love rises freely from your own heart. And so it does. Or does it? Your experience says that it comes from outside yourself—put there by God with your consent, as it says in *The Cloud of Unknowing.* Can it be that your longing love is but a reflection of God's love for you? Notice how often logic is contradicted when you let prayer rise from your heart.

No greater surprise hides in the transformations of spiritual growth than finding out that God is not about the business of making you smart, pure, or powerful, but loved and loving. In God's affection you are cleansed, centered, wakened, empowered, and bonded to God and to people in wholehearted loyalty and devotion. Your security rests not in your love for God, but in God's love for you. Your "work" in spiritual growth, therefore, is not to love God, but simply to be willing to be loved. For as you allow yourself to be loved, a longing love for God is awakened. Such wisdom in affection, indeed!

Fighting Against Unconditional Love

Allow the fact of your dependence on God's love for you to soak into your awareness and you will fight against it. You fight against the very gift you most want—the gift of unconditional love. Here, then, is another logical contradiction built into Christian spirituality. The fight against unconditional love comes to a head in the prayer-of-the-heart.

Sometimes you fight against God's love without even realizing what is happening. You stir up your willpower to obey God's commands but find that in obeying as a religious duty you lose the sense of delight in God's unconditional love. God becomes more tyrant than Lover. Another time you may fall into discouragement, feeling that other people experience God's love but not you. For you, God is either silent or "out to lunch." Again, you may decide that a painful experience proves God's anger toward you (or God's absence). You, then, refuse to use the pain to burn away your false pride, thereby staying closed to God's love. Spiritual pride is the most powerful weapon you can use to reject God's longing love. Many substitute their own spiritual heroics for simply allowing themselves to be loved. You know this is happening to you when you become highly critical of yourself and are not spontaneously loving toward others.

Loving God for God's Sake

A great wonder of interior prayer is that in being willing to be loved by God, your personal will begins to die and to be reborn as a will to love God above all—to be at one with, to enjoy and to praise God. The poet who began saying, "You have loved me with an everlasting love," marks a major change by ending the stanza confessing: "I knew I loved You when I could no longer find my own will Except arrayed in Your praise." Can you believe this? If this is not mere poetic language but true poetry—inspired utterance—you are seeing radical change for sure. You are hearing the words of a person who in truth is *being transformed.*

Radical change means change at the root. Let your will be lost only to reappear in adoring another and you have undergone root-deep change. Such changes happen in major upheavals. Your will for keeping up appearances, for personal achievement withers. You thrash about kicking over a career, a marriage, a pattern of work addiction. Gradually your will reappears in devotion to a simple life-style, to honesty in your relationships, to something bigger and more lasting than your own welfare, to a Reality that moves you, that holds you in awe and wonder. You find your own will again "arrayed in praise" of this Other Reality at work in you and beyond you. Even your transformation itself, as remarkable as it is, fades into the background of the Transforming One whose longing love has set the whole process in motion.

Being found as God's beloved does not end in blissful

adoration. You move on in the service of God's purposes in the universe. Longing love for God becomes a love of obedience to God. Obedience becomes your daily bread. Your love and will become one and the same. The fusion of love and will marks a new stage on the spiritual journey.

Bernard of Clairvaux, a great statesman of the twelfth-century church in France and master of the inner way, saw four stages of love as the milestones of spiritual growth:

First,	Loving self for self's sake
Second,	Loving God for self's sake
Third,	Loving God for God's sake
Fourth,	Loving self for God's sake

Praying with longing love marks the third stage: loving God for God's sake. A great leap occurs between stages two and three, from loving God for the sake of your security, your belonging, your self-esteem, and your spiritual self-development, to loving God for God's sake. In response to God's unconditional love a transformation of will and selfhood takes place. So radical is the change that the poet says,

> . . . even when there is no Joy
> I *will* to love you still. (Italics added)

The will that is working here is no bootstrap operation. Rather, it springs spontaneously from the center of a person. Such a will wakens at the touch of a transforming love. In turn, it transforms us into lovers—faithful, trusting, belonging, affirming, enjoying. It is a love-will that knows no bounds—neither race, sex, nor creed; neither toward neighbor nor toward God. Longing love has come full circle. As your love for God grows, so too does your sense of mystery.

A Priceless Treasure

At this point I want to share the entire final stanza of "A Song."

> You are my everything, my only aspiration,
> All the meaning of existence,
> My food and sleep and warming,
> The color and scent and touch of morning;
> And You are the night trailing its purpled‾
>   light
> Coming home to hearten my soul;
> Majesty reflected and mystery refracted
>   against my barricades
> In awful, bursting wonder.
> Thine the raptured agony of purity.
> Till I'm charred and ash consume me.
> I am not fire alone,
> We together burn as one.
> So Spirit and the Bride say, "Come,"
> Amen, Lord Jesus, Come—Ever Coming—
>   and Come . . .

Mystery is the theme of the final stanza. And not surprisingly. For mystery pervades the process of inner transformation.

To love God at this stage is to love God with single-mindedness:

> . . . my only aspiration,

and to experience and love God in everything:

> My food and sleep and warming,
> The color and scent and touch of morning;
> . . . the night trailing its purpled light.

Now comes the terror and the wonder of longing love:

> Majesty reflected and mystery refracted against
>   my barricades
> In awful, bursting wonder.

Words fail me now. Perhaps a story will do—about the thief who stole a priceless Oriental rug. On market day he hawked it for one hundred pieces of gold. A dealer in fine rugs recognized its value, paid the thief the one hundred pieces of gold at once, and when the rug was securely in his possession asked,

"How is it you sold this priceless rug for only one hundred pieces of gold?"

To this the thief replied, "Is there any number higher than one hundred?"

Could this story be a parable of today's well-to-do world? Is it possible to actualize your human potential, to enrich yourself by means of spiritual growth, and to come briefly into possession of the reality of unconditional love? But then, because its value so exceeds your ordinary ways of reckoning, could you be unable to comprehend its worth? Could you set about peddling your spiritual experience for the rewards of ego-satisfaction, for the healing of diseases, trading for psychic powers, or even for the image of a spiritual guide on the inner way?

Then comes the master collector of fine rugs with a question that breaks against your ego barricades "in awful, bursting wonder." You sense what you cannot say—that Longing Love devours and consumes like fire, and in consuming transforms, so that now

We together burn as one.

The pilgrim on the journey of inner transformation, "charred" but changed, now speaks with one and the same voice as the Spirit. A prayer leaps from the heart. Is it the poet's prayer or the Spirit's prayer? It is no longer possible to tell them apart. Together, burning with longing love as one, they pray:

Come,
Amen, Lord Jesus, Come—Ever Coming—
and Come . . .

What begins in the *doxa* of glorifying God and enjoying him in the experience of interior prayer becomes now, through further transformations of will and selfhood, a burning together as one, an intentional, will-full invitation to Jesus, the Christ, to consummate the love bond with God.

In the final chapter you will find a further discussion of the themes of being transformed in your will and of obedience on the inner way. Before pursuing the matter, however, I want to turn to our Lord's instruction on prayer. Just how does the tradition of interior prayer look when measured by Jesus' response to his disciples' plea, "Lord, teach us to pray"?

Lord, Teach Us to Pray

The central passage on prayer in all the Scriptures is found in Luke 11:1–4 and also in Matt. 6:9–13. The less elaborated passage in Luke is probably more as Jesus first spoke it.

Luke introduces the instruction by noting that Jesus "was praying in a certain place, and when he ceased, one of his disciples said to him, 'Lord, teach us to pray, as John taught his disciples' " (Luke 11:1). In Jesus' day, a spiritual teacher was expected to give his followers an inspired formula for prayer. The formula would open up for ordinary people the same path to God traveled by the spiritual master. Jesus did not challenge this expectation when asked to teach his followers to pray. Instead, he honored it by giving a model prayer:

> And he said to them, "When you pray, say:
> Father, hallowed be thy name.
> Thy kingdom come.
> Give us each day our daily bread;

and forgive us our sins, for we ourselves forgive
every one who is indebted to us;
and lead us not into temptation." (Luke 11:2–4)

This is not a Sunday morning prayer, although in Matthew's account it was expanded into a liturgical form. It is instead a whole course on prayer in a capsule. In the tradition of the rabbis, Jesus packed his teaching into a few easy-to-remember sentences. Every word is carefully chosen in such instruction. Even the sequence of sentences carries clues to unpacking our Lord's message about prayer. I shall discuss only one phrase of the model prayer here, since my purpose is to show its connection with the prayer-of-the-heart. (In my article in the *Review and Expositor,* Spring 1979, pp. 219–239, I have explored the entire prayer, phrase by phrase, looking at many ways in which interior prayer fits the intention of the model prayer. A few of the following paragraphs borrow from this earlier publication.)

Start at the Beginning

The first lesson to learn about prayer is that you need to start at the beginning. Where, then, is the beginning? Children (and some adults as well) begin with petitions—asking God for what they need and want. But the model prayer does not begin in "gimmies." Petition has its place: "Give us each day our daily bread" (Luke 11:3). But petition comes in the middle of the prayer, not at its beginning.

With more experience, you know that you do not begin prayer with your survival needs. You begin with spiritual needs. Yet Jesus put spiritual needs last—after survival needs: "Forgive us . . . deliver us . . . ." The really mature Christian knows that you begin in surrender to God. Right? Wrong again. Surrender is the theme of the second but not the first utterance in the model prayer: "Thy kingdom come" (Luke 11:2).

Where, then, do you start? The first word of the prayer is "Father." You begin *in relation* to God as Father, or, in our Lord's own word, *Abba* (Daddy). I have noted already that "abba" is the child's word for the male parent. Myron Weaver tells of being in the large, bustling lobby of New York's Metropolitan Museum of Art and seeing a small Middle-Eastern boy making a beeline for his father with the happy words trailing in his wake, "Abba! Abba! Abba!" ("A Life of Prayer and Holy Obedience," *Prayer and Holy Obedience in a War-wracked World,* p. 53, Papers from a Quaker–Southern Baptist Colloquy; Atlanta: Home Mission Board of the Southern Baptist Convention, 1982.) When you are separated from God, even for a moment, this is where you start. You make a beeline into his arms, calling, "Abba! Abba! Abba!"

How better can you make a beeline for God than to become still, silent, relaxed, centered, and then spontaneously from the heart to sing out the words, "Abba! Abba! Abba!" This is a perfect picture of the prayer-of-the-heart in action. In this way you start at the beginning. You begin not in petition, but *in relation.*

As I learned to enter prayer in this way, to begin in the experience of the Presence, I had some big surprises. I found that petitions and intercessions happen naturally and that so-called answers to prayer always come. Let me try to explain.

Petition Becomes Affirmation

Begin with interior prayer and everything else in the model prayer flows from that beginning. "Thy kingdom come" is no longer a petition wrung out of a struggle to surrender your will to God's will. It is, instead, an affirmation of a personal transformation already happening. The words carry the sense of "Thy kingdom *is coming* already."

"Give us each day our daily bread" is not now a petition either. It too becomes an affirmation: "You, Father, are giving us this day our daily bread." Since God is your Father, would he do anything other than meet your survival needs? Will a human father whose child asks for bread give a stone?

Likewise, "Forgive us . . . and lead us not into temptation" become affirmations of the reality of life in the Spirit—being forgiven, being guided, and being delivered from evil by the Father—"Hallowed be his name!"

The whole experience of prayer is transformed once you start at the beginning—in relationship, in enjoying the Presence. The aim of prayer changes from doing a religious duty to enjoying an intimate relationship. The style shifts from the petitional to the relational. The method becomes meditational rather than mental, nonverbal more than verbal, a prayer-of-the-heart rather than of the head.

You might suspect a bit of self-deception in my shifting the emphasis in the model prayer from petition to affirmation. You may wonder if I am going overboard into the power of positive thinking. Far from it. You must be absolutely honest with God about your pain and your hatreds of God as well as of others and of yourself. The prayer-of-the-heart may well be a cry of pain, a plea for help, a burst of tears over repeated failures. The point is that whatever comes, comes into the presence of the living God—and that presence makes all the difference.

Answers? Yes—Always!

Yet something more must be said. Strange as it seems, I find that the prayer-of-the-heart is answered—*always*. Remember, please, that I am saying this as a former skeptic about prayer who for more than two decades could not offer private prayer with integrity. But in the change from loving God for self's sake to loving God for God's sake, in the prayer-of-the-heart, answered prayer began to happen. I tend now to take the answers for granted. I receive them with joy and gratitude to God, but do not dwell on them, do not need them to strengthen my faith, and almost never speak of them. (For instance, I forgot to include a discussion of answers to prayer in my original planning for this chapter.)

Interior prayer produces not merely confidence but absolute certitude about the response. The certitude is not based on blind faith in scriptural assurances. It rests on the quality of your relationship with the Father, with your own Abba! Make your hopes and needs known to a loving parent or to a true friend and you know for certain that the parent or friend is now committed with you to the fulfillment of your goals. When they question the wisdom of your wants, you know their challenge comes out of goodwill and a desire for you to fulfill your true self. And so it is in relation to Abba.

A word from the poem we have studied comes winging back into focus: "So much wisdom is in that affection." Job found his answer to the problem of evil not in theological arguments but in the Presence of God coming to him out of a whirlwind. Lovers find the answer to life's emptiness in the love bond that unites them. Persons on pilgrimage in psychotherapy find their answers not in the advice of a therapist but in the quality of the relationship that develops between themselves and their therapist. Similarly a pilgrim on the inner way of spiritual growth receives answers to the deepest longing of the heart in the Presence of God, who transforms petitions into affirmations and needs into soul songs of gratitude and joy.

Intercession—the Flip Side of Petition

Intercession as well is radically changed when you pray with the mind in the heart. At first, as I studied the model prayer, I was puzzled as to why nothing is said about intercessory prayer. The New Testament is full of appeals to pray for one another and of reports of remembering one another in prayer. The problem dissolved as I thought about my experience in the prayer-of-the-heart. The clue in Jesus' model is in the plural pronouns: "Give *us* . . . forgive *us* . . . deliver *us* . . . ."

Take, for example, the petition "Give us each day our daily bread" (Luke 11:3). Attention to the food on your plate at mealtime—with the mind in the heart—expands into grateful awareness of all those who have had a part in growing, harvesting, processing, distributing, and selling it, not to mention those who prepare and serve it. Your awareness— and gratitude—expands to nameless persons on every continent of the globe. You are linked in the flow of life also with the animals and plants that die in order that you might live another day. The sense of your own finitude grows; you experience a deep readiness to spend yourself in serving others, and in due time to die as a gift to the ongoingness of life.

The sense of linkage with others takes form in gratitude on some occasions. At other times it forms in awareness of shared needs. Anxiety about surviving the threat of a nuclear holocaust flows by means of interior prayer into awareness of your mutuality of need with all who are similarly threatened. Concern for emotional well-being in family and work relationships links you to the needs of other family members and working associates. In whatever arena you may attend to your survival or spiritual needs, you discover yourself enmeshed with others in the same needs.

Who would have thought that intercession is the flip side of petition? I, at least, was taken by surprise to find that the deeper I plumb my own needs, the wider my sympathies expand toward others. In the prayer-of-the-heart I cannot avoid praying, "Give *us* . . . forgive *us* . . . deliver *us* . . . ."

Petition may waken your awareness of the needs of others or you may become burdened for another spontaneously out of direct contact. Given the desire to do so, how then do you pray the prayer of intercession?

In a word, you simply include the one for whom you wish to pray in your experience of the Presence of God. You may do so by visualizing the person or by silently calling the other person's name along with your own—calling you both into the Presence of the risen Christ. This assumes, of course, that you have learned the first lesson well, that you are relaxed, silent, and centered. You wait upon the Lord, and as you experience the Presence, you call into the Presence with you those for whom you wish to pray.

In Summary

We may say, in summary, that the prayer-of-the-heart is meditation in the service of loving God with a whole heart and your neighbor as yourself. It is a way of striking the cloud of unknowing with the sharp dart of longing love—love for God, love for others, and love for your true self! The prayer-of-the-heart fits our Lord's model prayer so well that I cannot help wondering whether they do not belong together. Could it be that the prayer-of-the-heart is necessary for praying in accordance with our Lord's model? Whether necessary or not, it is clearly compatible with Jesus' own experience of being at one with God and with his directions for praying to Abba, our Father.

Flowing from contact with the Father, from hallowing his name, is obedience to his kingdom, to his will, and, finally, discerning his will in the face of temptation and evil. Thus, obedience and discernment are the topics of the final chapter.

Chapter 5

And Then
It Gets More Difficult

The first lesson is the hardest, as we have seen, and after that it gets more difficult. The first lesson requires you to rely on your senses, but after that you move into a realm of nonsense. You are likely at first to say, "What's the *sense* of sitting still in body awareness?" Later, as the experience of Divine Presence opens you to specific changes in life-style, you may find yourself saying, "But that's *nonsense.*" Trusting your senses to lead you into the Presence of God is a hard lesson indeed, but trusting nonsensory divine guidance to lead you back into everyday living appears, at first, to make life much more difficult.

Obedience

On the other side of silence is the still, small voice of God calling for obedience. On the other side of Presence is divine demand. After praying, "Our Father," we are to pray next, "Thy kingdom come, thy will be done." The sequence in religious experience is always, "Trust *and obey.*"

Obedience Is a Dirty Word
For many people, obedience is a dirty word. It goes against your grain when you are fighting to be your own person. You

want autonomy, not submission; independence, not compliance; dignity, not dependence. Under a demand to obey, duty
is a burden and even an occasion for protest.

Alongside of obedience is another word: devotion. And
alongside of burden and resentment are privilege and gratitude. I remember my surprise on my first morning in London
when a waiter poured my coffee and then *he* said, "Thank
you." He brought my breakfast and setting it before me, *he*
again said, "Thank you." Later he removed my dirty dishes
and again *he* said, "Thank you." Although merely a convention today, the waiter's "Thank you" upon every act of service
echoes a time when going "into service" as a domestic was a
privilege, and gratitude was an appropriate response. Servants
were trapped in a closed social system where the best that
could happen to them to improve their lot in life was to be
chosen to serve in a "fine family." If all went well, they would
learn to obey, not out of duty, but out of devotion to the Lord
and Lady who entrusted their affairs to their care.

Indentured service is alien to life in a democratic society,
but the quality of relationship that prompts one person to
thank another for the privilege of serving is not. From
corporations to small businesses, from church staffs to federal
agencies, you can find junior-level officers who are wholeheartedly devoted to their superiors in the organization.
Awake to every wish of the boss, a loyal assistant feels
honored to serve. The heavier the responsibility piled on a
junior executive's back, the taller he or she stands. Sleepless
nights are devoted to the success of the company. Seventy-
hour weeks are spent eagerly, with high energy and good
spirits, and with nothing asked in return except the rewards of
service in a worthy cause with worthy colleagues.

Obedience need not be bought in such circumstances, for it

is sought. It is treasured, not resented. If demand is present at all in such obedience, it is self-demand—giving freely as to a chum, a dearly beloved neighbor, or a special friend. To obey in relationships such as these is not to be violated but to be actualized, not to be depleted but fulfilled.

How can obedience be both a burden and a joy? Does it not depend upon the quality of relationship with the person you serve? Let the person you serve be distant, impersonal, or harsh, and obedience is a burden; but let your superior be present, available, and aware of you, appreciating your gifts and your contribution to the cause, and your obedience is a joy.

Here, then, is a clue to overcoming the difficulty in spiritual growth of moving from enjoying the Presence of God to opting for obedience as your daily bread. The clue is twofold: (1) You trust a flow process in spiritual growth, from experiencing Presence to pledging obedience, and (2) you put your relationship with God above your need to serve others. You trust the relationship with God above your need to serve others. You trust the relationship to free you for spontaneous service. Trouble comes when you turn the formula around and pledge obedience to God in the hope of evoking the Divine Presence as a reward. Growth is stunted and service oftentimes sours when you plunge into service as a duty without enjoying the grace of unconditional love.

Several years ago, toward the end of a period of rapid progress in "the first lesson" of not-doing and not-knowing, I asked for guidance as to next steps. The question I put was this: "How may I continue to move toward wholeness, being open to the Spirit?" The response to my prayer surprised, pleased, and confused me all at once. The word that came was: "Relax and trust your spontaneity." "Relax" was not a word I wanted to hear. I wanted a new task. I wanted a call to more difficult spiritual disciplines. "Trust your spontaneity" was alien to both my temperament and my need to control behavior as a behavioral scientist. I wanted my personal life to be ordered and predictable as well. I welcomed the promise of a more relaxed and spontaneous life-style—someday. But in the main I looked away and let the "guidance" fade out of focus. Later, a hunger for obedience as my daily bread arose spontaneously. I remembered the earlier word, "Trust your spontaneity," and now I realize that spontaneity is the flip side of obedience. Let me try to bring out the meaning I have found in this connection.

Spontaneity, the Flip Side of Obedience

In Christian experience, spontaneity has been more feared than fostered. By definition, spontaneous behavior is "caused by natural impulse or desire." This is the problem, for who wants to give free reign to natural impulses and desires? Who, in fact, trusts natural impulses to be of use in spiritual growth even when held under tight rein? How can spontaneity, which is behavior caused by "natural impulse or desire," not planned beforehand and not under full conscious control, be trusted as obedience to God?

First, the function of natural impulse and desire in the spiritual life is not a new issue. It arises every time the new wine of the Spirit bursts the old wineskins of conventional religion. When Jesus defended his disciples for indulging their natural impulses and desire to eat on the Sabbath contrary to Sabbath laws, he offended the Pharisees, who were the champions of radical obedience to God (Mark 2:23–28). Next he entered a synagogue for worship and the

Pharisees asked him, "Is it lawful to heal on the sabbath?" He healed a man with a withered hand on the spot, saying, "It is lawful to do good on the sabbath." But the Pharisees began immediately to plot his death (Mark 3:1–6; Matt. 12:9–14).

Spontaneity-in-Love

Jesus literally put his life on the line in obedience to his natural impulse to do good to a fellowman. His obedience was spontaneity-in-love. He won the hatred of the Pharisees, for whom obedience meant the exercise of willpower in keeping the rules. The Pharisees were determined to force God to deliver them from foreign oppression by their radical obedience to religious rules. They had created a true majority in Israel for strict morality. They made radical obedience to God a political platform and won broad-based popular support for it. They believed in God with a passion. They were spiritually heroic. They stood on the power of will to control natural impulse and desire in the cause of doing God's will in human history—as they understood it.

Jesus understood God's will differently. He spontaneously indulged his natural impulse and desire to care for and to heal a wounded person. Then he met the Pharisees' test head on. In saying, "It is lawful to do good on the sabbath," he transformed obedience from an exercise of the will in the service of God's will (as interpreted by religious leaders) to a spontaneous indulgence of love in the service of people. He allowed human rather than institutional needs to define God's will.

The contest of willpower versus the spontaneity of love plagued the early church as well. The apostle Paul takes on the issue in his letter to the Galatians. Taking circumcision as a symbol of the religion of rules and willpower, Paul declares:

> For freedom Christ has set us free; stand fast therefore, and do not submit again to a yoke of slavery. Now I, Paul, say to you that if you receive circumcision, Christ will be of no advantage to you. I testify again to every man who receives circumcision that he is bound to keep the whole law. You are severed from Christ, you who would be justified by the law; you have fallen away from grace. For through the Spirit, by faith, we wait for hope of righteousness. For in Christ Jesus neither circumcision nor uncircumcision is of any avail, but faith working through love. (Gal. 5:1–6)

Paul is not blind to the risks of freedom in Christ, but he has discovered the obedience of a spontaneity-in-love:

> For you were called to freedom . . . ; only do not use your freedom as an opportunity for the flesh, but through love be servants of one another. For the whole law is fulfilled in one word, "You shall love your neighbor as yourself." (Gal. 5:13–14)

Having concluded his case for the obedience of spontaneity-in-love rather than of will and rule-keeping, Paul turns to the issue of discernment—to seeing clearly the differences between the works of the flesh and the fruit of the Spirit (see Gal. 5:16–25). Before we discuss discernment, however, we need to underscore a second point concerning obedience as spontaneity.

Spontaneity as Danger or Delight

Spontaneity can be both a danger and a delight. It can carry both death and life to the human spirit. Freedom in Christ can be used "as an opportunity for the flesh" or as the energy that ripens the fruit of the Spirit.

You need the wisdom of serpents and the harmlessness of doves in giving yourself to the obedience of spontaneity. The roots of destructive impulses may go very, very deep. For example, let a child grow up in a web of inconsistent parenting, allow the child's self-esteem to be put down brutally enough, and that child will be spontaneously malevolent—not merely a bad child, but an evil child. Let that child's twin be reared in a predictable environment, blessed with affirmation and graced with delight in parental eyes, and that child will be spontaneously benevolent—not just a good child, but a joy and a blessing to others.

In a safe and secure environment, a four-year-old girl is a good mother to her dolls. Let her world be torn apart by family crisis and dolls beware. She will be transformed into a terrible four-year-old mother. Battered and dismembered dolls will give mute testimony to the need to be secure in love in order to be spontaneously loving. Project this reality onto a cosmic screen and you see that in the spiritual life everything depends on your love bond with God. Obedience comes spontaneously only as you allow God to come upon you in unconditional love. You cannot force his love anymore than you can force the love of another person, but you can deepen your willingness to be loved. You can open yourself to God's coming. You can relax your fears of experiencing the Presence of God and trust yourself to respond to others in joy and love.

Willingness to Be Loved

The proper function of will in spiritual growth is not to be obedient. You do not will to be righteous. You do not will to be a spiritual athlete ready for competition in the Spiritual Olympics. Instead, *you will to deepen your willingness to be loved.* That is all. You simply will to be open to God's coming to you in love. You deepen your willingness. You allow God to come. You may allow God to come in a process of self-discovery through counseling. You may allow God to come into dialogue as you risk being honest about your fear, your hate, and your doubts about God. You may allow God to come in the persons of the wounded ones for whom you care. You allow God to come in the spontaneity of your impulses and desires. In it all you will only to deepen your willingness to be present to the Presence in whom you live and move and have your being. (For a thorough discussion of will and willingness in the spiritual life, see Gerald May, *Will and Spirit: A Contemplative Psychology;* Harper & Row, 1982.)

Spontaneity as Sacrifice

Surprising as it may be, spontaneity in the spiritual life is also the way of sacrifice. You sacrifice your will for self-indulgence, but this is only the beginning. Soon you begin to sacrifice the images by which you define yourself. Among them is the pride of mastering life on your own terms. If, in contrast, you live a hidden life, remain obscure and risk little, you sacrifice the safety of your well-worn ruts. You sacrifice your need to control other people. You give up the reins you hold on your career. You loosen your grip on your private dream for your marriage and your children.

All of this happens in a not-doing way. You do not decide that you *ought* to give up this or that bad habit. You do not then tear at yourself to change yourself in a passion to be obedient. You do not place your pleasures on the altar of self-sacrifice. Instead, in longing love for God and in enjoying the Presence of God you discover that old habits wither and drop away. Small turnings become in time major changes in your life-style. Subtle shifts occur in relationships with others. One day you realize that you have worked through an issue with someone without ever considering what you will get out of it. The joy of caring has crowded out your needs for power and personal advantage. Spontaneously you have sacrificed your self-will.

Then comes an even more radical sacrifice. You sacrifice your will for sainthood as well. Not many people admit a desire for sainthood in today's secular society, but just change the language slightly and see if you do not recognize yourself. Instead of sainthood, say: the desire for wholeness, a longing to get it all together, high ideals, and a twinge of self-satisfaction at being more serious and spiritually-minded than most of the people you know. Yes, you sacrifice all this as well.

Spontaneity may be the flip side of obedience, but spontaneity is layered deep. It can be love wrapped in fear or love casting out fear. So how do you know? How much do you risk when you sacrifice your will to a wholehearted willingness for God to come? Who can test the spirits of spontaneity to discern the spirit of truth and the spirit of error (I John 4:1–18)? One thing is clear: since obedience cannot be separated from discernment, things continue to get more difficult as you bring your longing for obedience and your trust in spontaneity to the task of discerning the will of God.

Discernment

Seeing Clearly (Discernment): The Twin of Obedience

Once upon a time a very religious man was walking beside a wide river. He was meditating on the law of the Lord, for he believed that if he kept his mind fixed on spiritual thoughts all the time, he would achieve perfection.

Just then his thoughts were broken up by the sound of a chant used in his religion to prepare for experiencing the Presence of God. He was angered by what he heard, for the chant was being done wrong. At each transition where one is supposed to say "ah-men," this man was saying "a-men."

He knew it was his religious duty to go to the man, who was probably a hermit living alone on the island in the middle of the river, and instruct him in the correct way to do the chant. You see how very religious and self-sacrificing he was, for he put his religious duty to care for an ignorant hermit ahead of his own quest for perfection.

So, renting a boat, he rowed across the river to the island, found the hermit moving in rhythm to his chant. "Friend," he said, breaking the hermit's concentration, "you are doing the chant wrong. I have come to instruct you in the right way."

"Thank you," said the hermit, genuinely grateful for the help he was being offered.

After instructing the hermit, he went away congratulating himself on his good deed. As he rowed back across the river, he recalled the ancient saying: "One who achieves perfection will walk upon the water without fear," and he dreamed of the day he would be able to walk on the water himself.

His meditation was interrupted, however, by the sounds of the hermit's chant once again. At the first transition, there came a faltering "ah-men," but as the chant progressed, the hermit lapsed back into his old habits, saying "a-men" over and over again. You can imagine how disgusted he was with the hermit. His thoughts about the ignorance of human beings and their persistence in error were interrupted suddenly by a strange sight. The hermit was coming toward him—walking on the water.

"I am sorry to bother you again," said the hermit as he approached the boat, "but I have forgotten the right way to say the chant. Would you be so good as to instruct me once more?"

Surprise! The story turns everything upside down. The

religious man is not wise after all, but ignorant. The hermit is not ignorant, but wise in his not-knowing. Religious knowledge is vain, and correctly done rituals are futile. Religious duties earn no merit, lofty aspirations confer no special powers. The secret of sainthood is hidden from the religious expert. It is known only to the hermit and to him only because he is wholly unselfconscious in his longing love for God.

Seeing the Difference Between Spontaneity and Studied Obedience

Discernment means to see clearly, to distinguish, to form good judgments. Discerning the will of God means seeing clearly in matters of obedience. First, as the story shows, it means seeing clearly the difference between spontaneity and studied obedience. It means distinguishing between the works of your will and the fruits of the Spirit—between willful obedience and willingness to be at one with God. The hermit was totally unselfconscious in his single-minded seeking to be at one with God. In contrast, his teacher was self-defined: he was religious, learned, virtuous, aspiring after spiritual place and special powers. The hermit had lost all self-definition. He was one with his longing for God. As a result, he walked on water without knowing that he was doing anything out of the ordinary.

Being spiritually "advanced" is heady wine, and it may become intoxicating. You can maintain your spiritual sobriety best by strengthening your ties to a religious tradition. Participating deeply in a community of faith and not needing to claim "advanced" standing as a spiritual pilgrim guards you against using either your freedom or your piety as cause for spiritual pride. Go overboard in the freedom of the Spirit and you may mistake the unitive experience of the Presence of

God for union with God (or, in psychosis, being God yourself). See yourself as a spiritual athlete who is climbing high on the mystical mountain and you may be suffering from spiritual narcissism. Gerald May defines spiritual narcissism as "the unconscious use of spiritual practice, experience, and insight to increase rather than decrease self-importance" (*Will and Spirit*, pp. 114–115). On the positive side, however, you may find that detachment from both images—the spiritually "liberated" and the spiritually "advanced"—allows you to love spontaneously in ways more effective than you have ever known.

One more caution is in order for you who are taking interior prayer seriously. To define yourself as a contemplative and to embrace discipline of the inner way as *the* way to God is also a greased slide into evil. First, you slide into the idea that with the techniques of meditation and interior prayer you can master your inner world. Next, you think you can master the outer world—through intercessory prayer, for example. Finally, when firmly in the grip of spiritual pride, you may presume mastery over God as well.

I discovered myself to be on this greased slide when I began to "use" meditation as a tranquilizer to cope with anxiety and tension states. During the prayer-of-the-heart I often lost self-consciousness and enjoyed the peace that passes understanding (Phil. 4:7). Naturally, I wanted to recover this peaceful state often, especially when upset about something. So I put my meditation techniques to work on my anxiety. Fortunately this did not work well at all. At first I could not see why I became more agitated during meditation when I was using it to allay anxiety. I experienced the deep peace only when entering it with little or no tension to begin with. Then I saw what was happening. I was using interior prayer as a tranquilizer. Instead of needing to tranquilize my anxiety, I needed to wrestle with it. I needed to let it be a messenger from God. I found that by facing it I could get a blessing from it, as when Jacob wrestled with the messenger of God at the river Jabbok (Gen. 32:24–29). Then I could go to interior prayer, enjoy the Presence of God, and praise him for coming not only in peace but also with a sword.

Doing the Ordinary in a State of Extraordinary Awareness

A second guideline in discerning the will of God is this: true spirituality involves doing the ordinary in a state of extraordinary awareness. Counterfeit spirituality is doing either the ordinary or the extraordinary in a state of ordinary, self-conscious awareness. Your state of awareness makes the difference. Ordinary awareness is self-conscious awareness. Extraordinary awareness is being present to the moment of experiencing. It is being free of self-consciousness. Extraordinary awareness is being present to a weasel in the wild, to a bird in a park, to a wildflower or a sunset, to a person or a machine, to sounds or body sensations, and, of course, to your longing love of God.

Brother Lawrence discovered in the seventeenth century that he could practice the Presence of God while washing pots and pans in the monastery kitchen. (See Brother Lawrence, *The Practice of the Presence of God the Best Rule of a Holy Life;* Fleming H. Revell Co., 1895.) A modern housekeeper may have an extraordinary awareness of a carrot while scraping it for dinner, or a transporting vision of a back fence while standing over the kitchen sink. Such awareness transforms ordinary household duties into moments of worship.

The extraordinary awareness central to spiritual growth is not lofty thought or visions. It is simply seeing traces of Spirit in the stuff around you. It is awareness of a "more" in ordinary happenings.

I once went to a retreat center to discern the will of God about a major vocational and geographical move. I listened for the still, small voice of God and heard a clear word: "I will feel more important if I move to the new position." Reject! This is an ego message. It is not worthy of a spiritual seeker's attention. So back to my praying I went to wait for some "worthy" impulse. But again the message came: "You will feel more important there."

I checked out my goals, my gifts, and my deepest longings. At heart I wanted most of all to continue traveling the inner way of spiritual growth that I had begun only a short while before. The "geography" of the move was of no real consequence! But that discovery did not help. If anything, it made the decision more difficult. So, back again to interior prayer— to wait and to listen. And again I heard: "Your ego needs will be better met in the new position." I fought back as before. Then in a quietly moving tide of joy and shame I accepted the word I kept hearing: "I am an ordinary person with ordinary ego needs. I give best when my ego needs are met. My calling is the same, whether here or there. Traveling the inner path is what matters for now, and that will be just as difficult and potentially as rewarding whether here or there. The 'geography' is truly of no consequence."

Here was an extraordinary awareness about an ordinary decision. The entire matter was shifted to an inner test of my will to travel the inner way of God-consciousness in the ordinary pursuit of self-conscious ego-satisfactions. Even now, nearly a decade later, I share this memory with a twinge of shame (at being ordinary, you see), and yet with a radiant heart of gratitude and joy. I knew then and I know now that I had found rock center. I could build on that rock and let the rain fall, the floods come, and wind beat upon that house and it would not fall "because it had been founded on the rock" (Matt. 7:24–27).

Certainty in Knowing

The third guideline seems almost beyond the reach of words to tell. It has to do with a quality of certainty in knowing what aids you in discerning the will of God. Let a teenager ask: "But how do you *know* when you are in love?" and most adults will reply: "Never mind. When it happens you will know. You will know." This is the answer I want to give when asked, "How do you know when inner guidance is from God?" Evil lurks at the door of such advice, however. For the door may be opened to a certainty that is dogmatic, rigid, and blind to all other considerations. An absence of "guidance" may invite despair about ever knowing anything for sure.

Perhaps the falling in love analogy is more than accidental at this point. When you are truly in love, you are open to questions and objections. You can hear them and look at them honestly without closing up. You do not have to take a parent's concerns as an attack on your maturity, your good judgment, or your freedom to choose for yourself. What is more, you can face separation from your lover without losing hope of eventual reunion. Separations may extend into months and years. Continents may divide you. But, if you are truly in love, you know with perfect certainty that your love will prevail. "Centered knowing" I shall call it.

In the Kew Gardens near London stands a magnificent gate to a Japanese temple—a gift from Japan to the British people. Facing the gate, as if to enter the temple, you see two lattice-type brass-work sculptures. On the right is a warrior mounted on horseback, tightly holding the reins. He is clad in armor, sword at his side. He rides confidently—proud and prestigious! On the left, as if leaving the temple, is the same man, stripped naked, clinging with bare hands and knees to the back of a sea serpent that is carrying him into the mysteries of the deep. The warrior on horseback has confidence. His confidence rests in his willful mastery of the world of ordinary experience. Leaving the temple, having been met by the living God, the same man, with a sea serpent between his knees, plunges into mystery in a state of "centered knowing." His self-image, with all the trappings of status and power, and his usual ways of coping with what lies ahead, have been stripped away. He is being carried into the deep by a power that he can neither control nor escape. He knows the sea serpent with a certainty beyond belief. His whole being is centered in the sea serpent, and this is "centered knowing."

In my father's final illness, he shared deeply about his spiritual journey. He told me of his awakening to Jesus Christ as Lord and then of his college years of wilderness wandering—a period of religious doubt. Then he added, "And all through those years of wandering I *knew* that Christ was giving me permission to wander." This too is "centered knowing." (The story of his being transformed in his middle years may be found in, Everett W. Thornton, *A Love That Heals;* Broadman Press, forthcoming.)

Do not read this to mean that true discernment eliminates fear, doubts, and worries in decision-making. Remember the naked warrior astride a sea serpent and the college youth wandering in a spiritual wilderness. Plunging into mystery stripped of familiar ways of ego mastery can be terrifying. So you press your knees all the harder into the sea serpent in a deeply "centered knowing" that you are on your way to the home of your soul. You need only a few such moments of discernment in a lifetime to stay on course. Do you still worry? Yes. Are you uncertain? To be sure. Yet at some level, beyond saying, you rest in a "centered knowing" that your discernment of God's will is true.

The Primacy of Love Over Will

Consider, fourth, what it means to see clearly the primacy of love over will and of unconditional over conditional love. No more moving story speaks to the themes of discernment and the primacy of love than the story of King Solomon and the two prostitutes each claiming to be the mother of the same child.

The two women "wrangled before the king." One said, "My son is alive, your son is dead." The other said, "That is not true. Your son is dead, my son is alive." Now hear the judgment of King Solomon.

> "Bring me a sword," said the king. . . . "Cut the living child in two . . . and give half to one, half to the other."

At this the woman who was the true mother pleaded with the king: "Give her the child; only do not let them think of killing it!" The other woman said, "He shall belong to neither of us. Cut him up."

> Then the king gave his decision. "Give the child to the first woman," he said, "and do not kill him. She is his mother." All Israel came to hear the judgment the king had pronounced, and held the king in awe, *recognizing that he possessed divine wisdom* for dispensing judgment. (See I Kings 3:16–28; italics added)

In one woman's cry, giving up her child, true love is revealed. In the other's calloused, "Cut him up," her self-will comes clear. Theirs is at first a contest of wills. Solomon transforms it into a contest of love against will. In her surrender of the contest the true mother appears. Love overcomes will. The mystery of birthing and of life supplants the will for the mastery of life. Because the king recognizes the primacy of love over will he is held in awe. His people *recognize "divine wisdom"* in his judgment.

Who does not recognize divine wisdom in the primacy of the unitive power of love over the divisive power of will? Is it any wonder that love is the power at work in being transformed and self-will a major block? The work of discernment requires you, therefore, to test the spirits of love and will and of unconditional and conditional forms of love.

On the inner way of spiritual growth spiritual and sexual experience may become confused. One reason for this is that a unitive experience with God wakens intense longings for unconditional love. When such love is aroused in the context of poor love relationships with other people, you are strongly tempted to seek fulfillment in a sexual way. When the other person also is longing for unconditional love, confusion rapidly grows. (Gerald May discusses sex and the life of the Spirit extensively and well. See *Will and Spirit*, chs. 6 and 7.)

Blocks to spiritual growth appear when you try to make the conditional love of family and friends take the place of the unconditional love of God. Bitter battles between parents and children and court battles between divorcing spouses are complicated by such confusion. Displace your longings for unconditional love onto your spouse and you have a setup for frustration. Frustration breeds anger and anger either erupts in blaming or goes underground. In either case the relationship goes sour. Worst of all, your willingness to be loved by God gets lost in the battle of wills with your spouse. What may have begun as a spiritual crisis gets transformed into a family conflict. Soon we feel that God is absent or cruel to let us be so miserable. At such a time spiritual growth may get badly stuck.

Seeing Beyond Your Self—Seeing the Face of Evil and the Back Side of God

You are not contained within your skin. Both the good and the evil that is in you is also outside you. You know that the air you breathe is both inside and outside your lungs. The music you hear is both inside and outside your ears. Your feelings too are both inside and outside you. Pay attention to your interpersonal world and you will find your feelings in the "atmosphere" to some extent. Walk into a room where people are either mad, sad, glad, or scared, and before a word is said you experience the feeling in the room. Even your thoughts are outside as well as inside you. Scientific discoveries regularly happen at about the same time in opposite corners of the world without direct exchange of information taking place. Mythic stories spring up and grow in different cultures and different languages but with similar plots and themes. Common features of human experience give birth to common thoughts, images, and understandings. "When one flower opens, ordinarily dozens open." And so, it would appear, does the human mind and spirit. (Quotation from *The Kabir Book,* tr. by Robert Bly, p. 27; Beacon Press, A Seventies Press Book, 1977.)

Seeing clearly in the spiritual life means seeing beyond your own skin—discerning the spirit of evil and the Spirit of God. My image: seeing the face of evil and the back side of God.

The lines of the face of evil are drawn by fear. Feeling weak and vulnerable in the world is not neurotic; it is realistic. Human beings are weak and vulnerable in the world. Many of the dangers that beset us come from outside us. Their proportions are sometimes cosmic; their impact evil. Few people see the face of evil, but everyone sees the face of fear. You see the face of fear when a face twists with alarm. You see the face of fear in the eyes of your friends at times, and also in a mirror. Sometimes you call it the face of death. Fear presses your panic button, prompting flight or fight. In flight you run away from mystery, freeze your spontaneity, retreat into ego control and try to master your own fate. Fight becomes a power struggle toward the same end—to predict and to control the world; to replace mystery with mastery. Religiously, fear changes devotion into duty, joy into rigidity, and a spirit of freedom and power into a dark force that saps your strength. Thus a vicious cycle begins: as you become drained by oppressive religion, your fears increase, demanding more control and kicking up more fears.

You see the face of fear on the rich man of our Lord's parable, who tore down his barns and built bigger ones (Luke 12:13–21). He then said to himself: " 'Soul, you have ample goods laid up for many years; take your ease, eat, drink, be merry.' But God said to him, 'Fool! This night your soul is required of you.' " Fear does not allow you to be merry. Fear withers up your soul.

For years, I interpreted this parable to be about the workaholics of the world who retired rich only to be zapped by heart attacks before they could enjoy their wealth. But in the passage, "This night your soul is required of you," the word for "soul" is not *bios,* physical life, but *psychē,* your totality as a person, your true self. The parable points to a process by which a decision to seek security in material things automatically withers the soul. Fear dictates a decision to make yourself rich. In yielding to fear, you lose the opportunity to make your *self* rich, that is, to discover the joy of being centered in your true self, or being at one with God.

The parable points also to the temptation to tear down the barns of international interdependence and build bigger barns (called silos) in which to store nuclear-tipped missiles. Is it possible that a nation's soul may atrophy under a policy that places top priority on military might?

Here, then, is a basic guideline for discernment: when fear prevails in a decision-making process, you are seeing the face of evil. When love prevails, you are seeing the hand of God. For "there is no fear in love, . . . perfect love casts out fear. . . . He who fears is not perfected in love" (I John 4:18).

The face of evil can be seen in fear, but no one can see the face of God. God is absolute mystery, and mystery is beyond knowing. God is love, but not everything veiled in mystery is loving. God is Spirit, but so is evil. God is light, but so is nuclear holocaust (as Chaim Potok has shown in *The Book of Lights;* Alfred A. Knopf, 1981; Fawcett Book Group, Crest Books, 1982). The problem is that you can never see the face of God. You never see God coming. You only see God going—you see God's back side. How much easier it is to make a positive identification when you see a person's face.

The image of God's back side comes from Exodus 33. Moses returns from Mt. Sinai with the Commandments carved in stone only to find the people dancing around a golden idol of their own making. In a rage, Moses smashes the tablets, orders the slaughter of three thousand of his own people, and collapses in fear—the fear that God will be with them no longer. But God does not leave Moses alone. God continues to prompt him to lead the people on to the Promised Land. So Moses prays for reassurance, saying, "Show me your glory, I beg you."

And God says: "You cannot see my face; . . . for man cannot see me and live. . . . Here is a place beside me. You must stand on the rock, and when my glory passes by, I will put you in a cleft of the rock and shield you with my hand while I pass by. Then I will take my hand away and you shall see the back of me; but my face is not to be seen" (Ex. 33:18–23).

Since only the back side of God may be seen, how may we discern that it is God who has passed by? The back side of light is shadow. The back side of fire is cold ashes. The back side of life is death. And the back side of love is—fear: *the very face of evil.* Could it be that discerning the back side of God requires paying attention to the shadow side of life, to the cold ashes of despair, to the reality of death? Must a person look into the eyes of evil itself in order to see God truly?

I found a way into this mystery some years ago when visiting the Rothko Chapel in Houston, Texas. The chapel is dedicated to the worship of the One God by all the faith groups of planet Earth.

Immense canvases, stretching from floor to ceiling, cover each wall of a concrete structure. The paintings are the work of the late Mark Rothko of New York City. Commissioned by the John de Menil family of Houston, Rothko was invited to express a vision common to the religious spirit of all humankind. During my visit, the space within the chapel's walls was totally empty except for a wooden bench beneath a skylight in the center of the structure.

Entering, I was stunned by what I saw. Every face of the chapel seemed to be hung in black. I stumbled forward to the bench and fixed my eyes on the canvas before me. Slowly, as my eyes adjusted to the light, I saw emerging out of the blackness deep brownish and purplish reds in patterns of exquisite variety, complexity, and energy.

As stated by Mrs. John de Menil at the opening of the chapel (February 27, 1971), Rothko brings us to "the threshold of transcendence, the mystery of the cosmos, the tragic mystery of our perishable condition. The silence of God, the unbearable silence of God." As Elijah heard the still, small voice of God in the silence that followed the storms, so for me, on a day in 1972, the mystery in Rothko's art whispered a bit of its secret as I allowed myself to be present to the blackness of the canvas before me. Words never do justice to such a moment, of course. But in the words of the present discussion, Rothko's canvas said, "Attend to the black face of evil, for even there you may see—in blood-red outline—the back side of God." It was so, and I came to know in the way of not-knowing something more of God's glory.

Another identifying mark on the back side of God is humor. I missed the humor on my first visit to the Rothko Chapel. My first impulse was anger. I wish now I had laughed. Here was a fortune in concrete and canvas. Here, too, was a great expectation: the promise of a spiritual vision for the space age located in Space City, U.S.A. And it all came to an empty room, a wooden bench, and concrete walls draped in black. Over the years the link between tragedy and comedy has become for me bigger and stronger. The blood-red patterns in Rothko's canvases reveal God's unconditional love in the blackness of human ignorance and lostness. The simplicity of the chapel exposes religious pretense and the folly of human aspirations to penetrate the mystery. The chapel calls for awed silence and belly laughter all at once.

God comes to you in the blackest of times. You see God's back side—nothing but God's shadow. You know you have a fight on your hands. This is spiritual warfare and the stakes are high. You are caught up in a life-or-death struggle. Still, you do not need to be grimly serious. You know that in time you will see the absurdity of your anxiety. Then, at last, you laugh again. You laugh the whole-bodied laughter that transforms defeat into spiritual victory.

Now put yourself into this situation: you are on retreat trying to learn how to relax, center your mind, and meditate. You try hard, but the more you try, the more trouble you have with distractions and drowsiness. Then the retreat leader says in a solemn voice: "There are three steps in overcoming distractions and drowsiness." You grit your teeth and brace yourself for another task. The leader says:

> First, you quit trying.
> Second, you quit trying to quit.
> Third, (a long pause) you quit quitting.

The leader's demand soaks in slowly. When it does, you throw back your head and roar. As the laughter fades away, you go back to sitting in silence—and this time it happens. You see the blood-red patterns of meaning in your blackness. You also see the absurdity of trying to master mystery by the techniques of meditation.

My father faced the black canvas at age fifty-seven during an ambulance trip to a coronary care unit. Later he tells of that ride:

> I feel a distinct, certain knowing that I am going
> out there. I am afraid. I am in a state of panic. I
> know I am going out there. I know that suddenly I
> will meet Him, and I wonder, "Is He friendly?"

I too rode in that ambulance, holding his hand. I was a middler seminarian home for the holidays. What I can add to the story is that he spoke of his fear to me. I gave him glib reassurance that of course God is friendly. And with great force he gasped, "How do *you* know?" And I was dumbstruck.

Thirty years later I stood by his bed during his final illness. We shared many things in the early hours before hospital routines got in the way. One morning he recalled our ambulance ride thirty years before and said:

> You know, later it came to me one day that Peter must have met me at the gate of heaven during that ambulance ride. He looked me over and gave his order: "He's not a keeper. Throw him back. Maybe he will grow some more."

Then, looking me in the eyes with quiet confidence and obvious enjoyment of the fishing imagery which he knew I would appreciate, he added:

> And I know that I have grown spiritually in the thirty years since that day. I believe he will find me to be a keeper this time.

(The story is told more fully in *A Love That Heals*, previously cited.)

So, there it is again: a healing sense of humor bringing out the patterns of meaning in the black canvas of impending tragedy. Could humor be the key to discerning the will of God when you can see only God's back side? I wonder.

Conclusion

The kingdom of heaven is like treasure hidden in a
field, which a man found and covered up; then in
his joy he goes and sells all that he has and buys
that field. Again, the kingdom of heaven is like a
merchant in search of fine pearls, who, on finding
one pearl of great value, went and sold all that he
had and bought it. (Matt. 13:44–45)

The parables of the treasure and the pearl have several
things in common. Both show persons going about their work
in the world. They are ordinary people—not famous, not
well-to-do, not special in any way. Both are surprised to
discover a treasure hidden in the stuff of everydayness.
Neither one can possess the treasure on finding it. Excitement, yes. Joy, yes. But not ownership—not yet. Both must
sell all they have in order to buy the treasure they have found.
They do sell it all, and in the end they do own the treasure
and the pearl of great value.

Jesus told these parables to help people know what the
kingdom of heaven is like. As you pay attention to the
parables, you prepare yourself for both the transforming
moments of awakening and discovering and the long journey

of risking all in order to own your heavenly treasure.

I have written this book in the hope that some readers who plow through books because they have to will have discovered a treasure hidden in these pages. I hope other readers who pick up books like this in search of pearls of wisdom will have found the one pearl of great value. I know well that discovering and owning are not the same experience. Selling all you have takes time. I know, too, that if you have discovered the treasure hidden here, your transformation will begin *in joy*. Without joy in the prospect of cashing in all your previous "treasures," you have not yet discovered the one of greatest value.

One final word needs to be said as you go about the work of selling off your blemished pearls in order to own the perfect one. Be as inconspicuous as possible. The person who buys a field at a cost equal to an entire estate has to move very carefully· in the real estate world in order not to arouse competition for the treasure. Similarly, a pearl merchant cannot wipe out an entire inventory without stimulating rivalry among other gem collectors unless the merchant conceals his excitement in a low-key manner. So, in getting rid of your blemished values in order to own the perfect one, be as inconspicuous as possible.

In discovering your heavenly treasure, you join a spiritual underground. You must continue to live in an open way so far as your public life is concerned—maintaining your ordinary work in the world. But on the inner way of spiritual growth, you know that you are being transformed. On the inner way, your experience is extraordinary and your heart sings for joy. In due time you will own the field free and clear. The perfect pearl will be yours. Then you can go public. In the meantime keep a low profile and allow your inner pearl to grow within a shell of privacy. Stay open to the possibility of finding a small group of persons who are also cultivating priceless pearls, but protect the privacy of the group as well.

In the pearl market today, it takes seven years to cultivate a pearl of value. The analogy fits spiritual pearls as well. At least seven years is what it takes on the inner way between discovering and owning the treasure, for the treasure is your own true self. The trade-off is giving up your lust for mastery in order to be possessed by the lure of mystery. You sell off your will to be religious in order to buy the willingness to be loved by God. Like the ignorant hermit who walked on water without knowing he was doing so, you too will be transformed without making work of it. Perhaps your best clue that a dramatic change is taking place will be that strange, quiet, yet persistent sense of joy.

Questions for Thought and Discussion

1. What were you hoping to get out of this book? In what ways were your hopes met and how were they left unmet?

2. If you were to write your story of being transformed, what would your experience say to guide others that is not said here?

3. What do you make of the claim that relaxation and body awareness open the door to the Holy Spirit? What life-style changes would happen if you were to do "not-doing," as described in Chapter 3?

4. Suppose you were to take "not-knowing" seriously, i.e., seeing and feeling God through longing love. What life-style changes would happen gradually?

5. Do you ever fight against trusting in unconditional love? What would it take to tip the balance from fearing to trusting God's unconditional love?

6. If you gave free reign to spontaneity-in-love, how might you offend stern and proper religious people? How can you avoid using your freedom "as an opportunity for the flesh"?

7. What meanings have emerged for you out of black times? What humor? What have you learned about how to discern the hand of God in dark times?

8. Looking back, when have you known the joy of the parable (Matt. 13:44)? Looking ahead, how badly do you want it? Right now, are you willing to be unconditionally loved? Can you believe that the rest will take care of itself?

Notes